# AN IRONMONGER'S TALE

Gerald Leeke, managing director of the Leekes Group, and his mother Mrs Myra Leeke pictured in 1997 with a portrait of founder JH Leeke and, behind, Gerald's father and previous managing director Llewellyn Leeke

# An Ironmonger's Tale

## The Story of Leekes,
### a South Wales Family Business

DAVID LEEKE

Published by David Leeke.

*First Impression – 2007*

ISBN 978 0 9556102 0 2

© David Leeke

*Printed in Wales at
Gomer Press, Llandysul, Ceredigion SA44 4JL*

To my parents, grandparents
and, in particular, my brother Gerald,
who have given me the inspiration
to tell this tale.

Author David Leeke

# Contents

# Acknowledgements

To John David, who so readily agreed to help me in writing this book and who accompanied me on trips to the Rhondda, including a visit to 178 Court Street where it all started and where we were given a warm welcome by the lady who now lives there. We also visited the various Leekes stores to talk to people who have known the Leeke family and business over the last 70 years. Without his help in putting together much of this book we would never have been in a position to publish.

To my cousin Clive Davies who supplied the family tree and all the research for Chapter 1, including a number of photographs. He also checked the early chapters.

To Teresa Deeley and Melanie Evans in the administration of this work, and especially Ann John who has painstakingly helped with the transcript.

To Phil Carradice, the author of many books, for advice on so many aspects of writing and publishing a book.

To Peter Walker, who so readily agreed to allow me to quote from his recently published autobiography *It's Not Just Cricket* and Adrian Davies for lending me some photographs for use in this book.

To Paul Beddoe and the Leekes marketing department for their help with design and photography.

To Emrys Jenkins for his kind permission to use one of his photographs of Dunraven Street.

To Annabel Lloyd for her help in amending the manuscript.

To my wife Jeanette for all her help and support in so many different ways.

To so many family members, who have helped me in numerous ways. There are too many to mention individually.

To members of staff past and present who have taken time to talk to me about their experiences working for Leekes, many of whom feature in the book.

David Leeke
April 2007

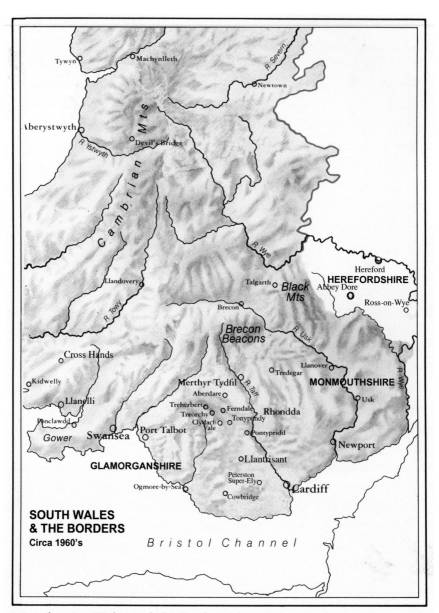

Map showing Wales and the Borders where James Leeke was from and began the business

# Foreword

When David asked me to help put together the story of his family, and particularly the story of the Leekes business, I really had no idea where this would take us. Everyone in South Wales knows the Leekes Group in some way, perhaps through visiting one of the stores or through the Vale Resort. I also knew a little of the family, having been at school with Gerald and having played rugby with both Gerald and David as youngsters at Pontyclun.

What I did not appreciate was the family effort that had been put into their successful businesses for over a hundred years. Few local businesses survive that length of time and even fewer family concerns can actually keep together through the pressures of economic depression, two World Wars and, I suppose inevitably, the odd difference of opinion!

Yet the story is not concluded. The family management of and interest in the business through James's grandchildren Gerald, Stuart and Diane – and their own children – are now stronger than ever. The emerging Hensol Castle project is today only in its embryonic phase.

Goodness knows what next initiative or adventure Gerald and his team will introduce to test the next generation of Leekes. Whatever it may be, I suspect the opening decades of this century will be equally as challenging as those of the last when James and Gwen Leeke decided to open a shop in the Rhondda.

John David
April 2007

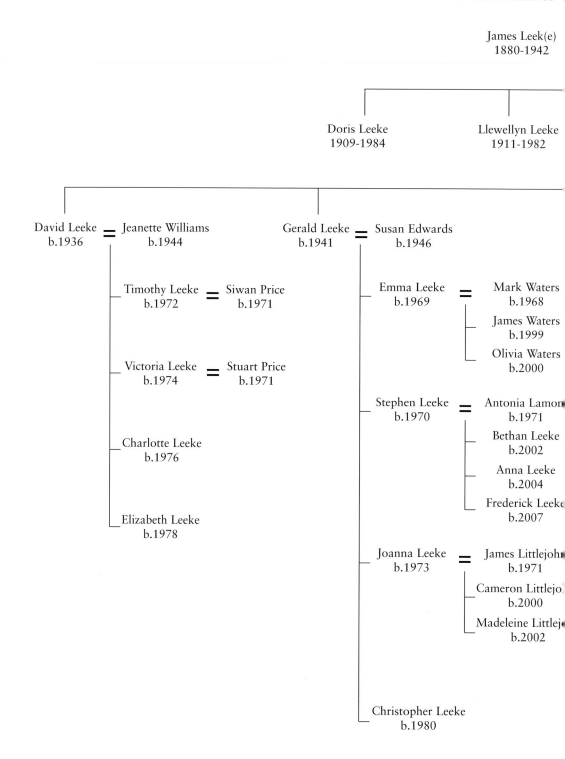

James Leek(e)
1880-1942

Doris Leeke
1909-1984

Llewellyn Leeke
1911-1982

David Leeke
b.1936
=
Jeanette Williams
b.1944

Gerald Leeke
b.1941
=
Susan Edwards
b.1946

Timothy Leeke
b.1972
=
Siwan Price
b.1971

Emma Leeke
b.1969
=
Mark Waters
b.1968

James Waters
b.1999

Olivia Waters
b.2000

Victoria Leeke
b.1974
=
Stuart Price
b.1971

Stephen Leeke
b.1970
=
Antonia Lamon
b.1971

Bethan Leeke
b.2002

Anna Leeke
b.2004

Charlotte Leeke
b.1976

Frederick Leeke
b.2007

Elizabeth Leeke
b.1978

Joanna Leeke
b.1973
=
James Littlejoh
b.1971

Cameron Littlejo
b.2000

Madeleine Littlej
b.2002

Christopher Leeke
b.1980

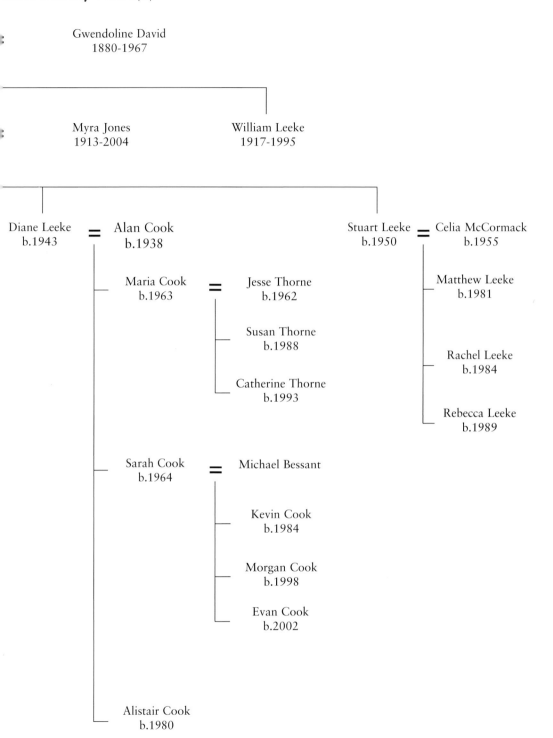

Gwendoline David
1880-1967

Myra Jones
1913-2004

William Leeke
1917-1995

Diane Leeke
b.1943

Alan Cook
b.1938

Maria Cook
b.1963

Jesse Thorne
b.1962

Susan Thorne
b.1988

Catherine Thorne
b.1993

Sarah Cook
b.1964

Michael Bessant

Kevin Cook
b.1984

Morgan Cook
b.1998

Evan Cook
b.2002

Alistair Cook
b.1980

Stuart Leeke
b.1950

Celia McCormack
b.1955

Matthew Leeke
b.1981

Rachel Leeke
b.1984

Rebecca Leeke
b.1989

# Introduction

Being the eldest grandchild I was named, with the addition of David, after my grandfather, James Henry Leeke. I was sent, on his recommendation, to Hereford Cathedral School for my education, which is near to where he was born and brought up and spent his retirement. With his humble beginnings he would probably have admired the school and its pupils from afar.

I have been interested in the history of my family for many years, and have always been involved in the business, and, looking back, I've been amazed by the way it has progressed, especially over the last 30 years.

My cousin Clive Davies, who now lives in Australia, is our self-appointed family historian and has traced our genealogy back to the early 18th century. His knowledge is truly encyclopaedic and I am sure he will one day publish a comprehensive family history.

However, this is the story of the family business which, of course, is inextricably linked with many of my family members since the early part of the last century, but especially with my grandfather James Henry Leeke, my father Llewellyn Leeke, and my younger brother Gerald. They have been the conductors orchestrating a choir of thousands who have contributed to the success of Leekes throughout a century of business in South Wales and beyond.

Although my own career developed separately from the family business I have always retained some peripheral interest. Yet it was not until the story was recounted in this book that I really fully realised what an achievement those other family members had made: firstly in surviving as businessmen and women throughout all the turmoil of the last hundred years and, secondly, in consolidating that survival through expansion and diversification, particularly in the last 30 years, to create one of South Wales' best-known and respected companies.

Why did I want to publish this story?

As the eldest of James's grandchildren I can still remember my grandfather during my visits to Oakdene Court in Herefordshire and, also, our days in Court Street, Tonypandy where I and my family lived until I was thirteen years old. Subsequently I was heavily involved in Dunraven Street during my school holidays until 1955 and thereafter at weekends in both Dunraven Street and Station Yard until Father's death in 1982. Although he had always made it clear he wanted Gerald to succeed him he was always keen for me to be fully involved when time permitted. I was always, at his request, able to take time off work to run the business in Tonypandy when he was on holiday. I can remember helping him with his accounts when he always, without fail, paid his bills at the end of the month to obtain his settlement discount without ever needing an overdraft.

When I became a partner at local accountants Williams Ross in 1965 I took over the preparation of the annual accounts and all the tax and financial planning, including the family tax returns. I continued to do this until I retired from the practice in 2000 when, due to the rapid expansion of the company during the 1990s, the decision was taken to appoint Deloittes, one of the country's top accountancy firms, to obtain more specialised advice.

I suppose it was my retirement that consolidated my view that the story of the Leekes business was worth publishing and, early in 2003, I discussed the prospect of producing this book with John David whom I had known since our rugby-playing days together in the early Sixties. John had published histories both of his own family and the local rugby club at Pontyclun in the past and was immediately able to highlight the many pitfalls in such a project. Needless to say I was delighted when he agreed to assist in writing this book. We have managed to distil hundreds of family and business anecdotes down to a story that could well have a broader interest than solely for my own family.

Finally I would like, once again, to thank the many employees of Leekes, both past and present, who have contributed some of their memories for this publication. Without them there would have been no business and consequently no story to tell.

David Leeke, April 2007

# Chapter 1

# SEEMS LIKE A GOOD PLACE TO START

The Leeke family roots have been reliably traced back to Elizabeth Leek who was born in North Herefordshire in 1776. The surname appears in official documents from the 18th and 19th centuries variously as 'Leek', 'Leak' or 'Leake'. At this time the spelling of surnames was frequently left to the whim of a parish or census official as the majority of working people were illiterate. We also know from family research that the name 'Leeke' appears on the Herefordshire/Shropshire border as early as the 13th century. We know from early census and parish records that, in the main, the family's roots were firmly based in agricultural work.

The Leys at Barewood, Herefordshire – birthplace of James Leek

As far as the family business is concerned, however, the story starts with James Leek who was born on 24th July 1880 at The Leys, Barewood, near Pembridge in Herefordshire. He was the tenth and youngest child of William Leek, a labourer who had married 18-year-old Mary Jones at Pembridge in July 1858.

Following William's death in 1883 the family generally dispersed and three-year-old James lived for a time with his second sister Alice and her husband James Footitt nearby in Ross-on-Wye.

The Old Forge in Walton, Radnor where James Leeke served his apprenticeship

James officially acquired a middle name – Henry – and the final 'e' to his surname between the 1891 census and the start of his apprenticeship four years later. At the age of 15 he began a three-year apprenticeship for John Lucas of Walton in the county of Radnorshire. His contract stipulated that *"he be taught the art of black-smithing and shoe-smithing forsaking taverns, play houses and dice tables. The contracting of matrimony was forbidden"*.

James's eldest brother William – who had assumed the role as family head after the death of their father – put up a non-repayable bond of £10. The young apprentice was to be provided with *"meat, drink, tools, washing, lodging and all other necessaries and two shillings weekly"*.

James and another apprentice were boarded with a smallholder and his wife and were kept on meagre rations. The smallholders used to slaughter their lambs very fat and make candles from the tallow. The boys believed the cawl (soup) they had for supper was made from candle-grease and water – one swish around with the candle through the week and two on Sundays. On market days they were left with some bread and cheese to fend for themselves. On one such day they decided to even up the score by collecting all the eggs they could find and hard boil them. They then had a contest to see who could eat the most. Determined and competitive, James ate between 15 and 18 and was 'thoroughly bound up' for a week!

On completion of his apprenticeship in 1899 James volunteered to serve in the Boer War in South Africa in the Royal Army Medical Corps as a stretcher-bearer and cook. It is believed

James Leeke's Boer War medal. The rim is engraved with '13388 J. LEAKE R.A.M.C.'

he was invalided out with enteric fever, but he would later claim he never saw a Boer or a bullet! Although the records of Boer War veterans who survived are extremely scant, James's self-deprecating claim seems highly unlikely.

James Leeke in the Medical Corps during the Boer War (first left in the back row)

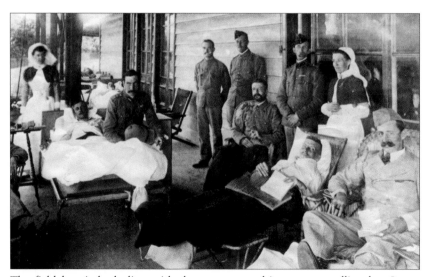

The field hospitals dealing with the troop casualties were appalling but James Leeke could not have missed the fact that the officers received far superior medical treatment

When the war ended at the beginning of the new century, it had claimed the lives of 5,774 British troops and some 4000 Boers and left 22,829 Britons wounded with the limited medical support utterly overstretched. The experience would have had a profound effect on the 20-year-old Jim Leeke. The treatment and evacuation of casualties was crude and badly organised, as were the steps to combat the ever-present threat of disease by the lack of field hygiene. Dysentery, enteric and typhoid took a heavy toll, with far more British troops lost through fever than from the bullets of the Boers.

After his military service James followed his trade of blacksmith. He first worked in Bluecoats Street, Hereford before brighter prospects attracted him to South Wales where wages were higher, boosted by the booming coalmines. He worked briefly in Merthyr Tydfil where he sharpened miners' tools. The *Morning Chronicle* describes the role of blacksmiths at collieries at that time:

> *"The miner possessed his own picks and drills – at least half a dozen picks – and he was personally responsible for keeping them fettled . . . a blacksmith, partially paid by the colliery, keeps the iron part in order. The picks have to be sharpened every day, so each hewer when he ascends goes straight with this implement to the blacksmith's shop, and next morning finds it laid out in readiness for him. The hewer paid 2d a fortnight for this service."*

The early 1900s saw James Leeke move from Merthyr to the village of Peterston-super-Ely in the Vale of Glamorgan. Here he assisted in building the White Bridge which, today replaced by a footbridge, spanned the River Ely near The Sportsman's Rest pub, connecting a newly-built residential area with the old village. It originally formed part of an ambitious vision of South Wales coal-owner and philanthropist John Cory of Duffryn whose statue graces Cathays Park in Cardiff city centre.

John Cory owned the mainly agricultural land which made up the southern part of the village. He was influenced by the Garden

The Sportsman's Rest at Peterston-super-Ely (early 1900s)

Suburb Village movement instrumental in the development of places like Bournville and Welwyn and planned a similar development at Peterston, to be known as Glyn Cory. The scheme envisaged homes for about 6,000 people, a park, golf course and other amenities. Only a fraction of this grand scheme came to fruition, which is the village's pleasant and leafy residential area of Wyndham Park today.

Whilst working at Peterson-super-Ely James won the heart of Gwen David, the daughter of a carpenter and contractor, William J David (1852-1926), from Baglan near Port Talbot. She had been assisting her mother's sister, Gwen Baker (nee Roderick, 1866-1950), the landlady of The Sportman's Rest and, later, The Three Horseshoes, just up the road.

James Henry Leeke and Mary Gwendoline David were married at Baglan Parish Church on 4th July 1908. His occupation was given as a *Smith*, his place of residence was now given as *Llwynypia (Rhondda)* and his father described as *William Leeke (deceased), Gardener.*

They set up home at 178 Court Street, Tonypandy, on the road to Clydach Vale, a typical terraced house on a steep hill above Tonypandy Square. James initially operated a smithy for sharpening tools at the rear of the house and then opened a small ironmongery business in the front room.

The wedding of James Henry Leeke and Mary Gwendoline David on 4th July 1908 (bride, seated, centre, with her bridegroom standing to her right)

That early family business was, in all senses, the start of it all. The considerable commercial successes that followed in the latter part of the last century can all be traced back to this small front room in Court Street. So why the Rhondda, why Tonypandy and why even Court Street for a young Herefordshire blacksmith and his new wife from Baglan?

There were relatives living nearby but the real key to James's decision to relocate here was the availability of well-paid work due to the vitality of the Rhondda, which was founded on the continuing demand for high quality coal.

The economic growth of the Rhondda Valleys in the 40 or so years up until the 1920s is well-documented: a mainly agricultural population of some 1000 people in 1851 had swelled to 152,781 by 1921. In the decade 1901 to 1911, James and Gwen Leeke were among the 38,000 new settlers. It was a Klondike-style rush for a better life, comparable perhaps to the surge for gold and diamonds which was a fundamental part of the backdrop to the Boer War from which James had so recently returned.

People were accommodated in either colliery-managed or speculatively-built, terraced houses that clustered around each pithead. Although each community often had fiercely conflicting traditions, the area developed its own way of life and social culture that had a great energy.

1908 – the same year that James and Gwen were married – saw a number of significant developments in the Rhondda Valleys. Electric tram services operated by the Rhondda Tramway Company were introduced into the two valleys and some 50 tramcars and 300 employees brought a unique improvement to public transport facilities. This service, plus the Taff Vale Railway's opening of a station at Tonypandy, could only be good news for local retailers.

The same year saw the first ever rugby league international between Wales and England played at Tonypandy before a 12,000-strong crowd as well as a match between the touring Australian rugby league side and one representing Mid-Rhondda.

Just one year on the town's Empire Theatre opened, as did its Judge's Hall dedicated to Judge Gwilym Williams of Miskin Manor, whose family had contributed most to its construction. 1909 was also a big year for James and Gwen personally with the birth of their first child, Doris, on 25th May, whose birth certificate described James as a *"blacksmith and ironmonger (master)"*.

The commercial and social attractions would have been irresistibly exciting to James and Gwen Leeke. Throughout Britain these were prosperous years before the horrors of the First World War which began in 1914: even the middle classes dressed for dinner, and in the provinces clerks and shopkeepers worked hard and lived well.

While Tonypandy's Dunraven Street and De Winton Street made up the commercial centre of the lower Rhondda, Court Street was very much the retail centre of the adjacent Clydach Vale and Blaenclydach areas. The three Cambrian pits at the very top of that community employed over 4000 men, and in Court Street they were serviced by a wide range of shops before the war years took their toll. Kelly's 1914 Street Directory lists grocers, drapers, butchers, fruiterers, a dairy, hairdressers, milliners, bookmakers and furniture dealers. For the cultured, Miss Frances Jones Tudball taught music at number 63. The Mid-Rhondda Working Men's Club and Institute – popularly known as The Monkey Club – at number 175 was a source of refreshment and debate. Dr Jeremiah Sheeton had a surgery at number 21 and A. Williams & Sons were undertakers at number 219. Next door to James and Gwen's home and ironmongery shop Arthur Whitsun had a furniture business at number 179. For the less adventurous it was possible to be born, live and die in Court Street without ever needing to leave!

The couple maintained close ties with James's older sister, Martha (Mart), and her husband Robert Challinor, who had moved shortly after them to Trealaw in the Rhondda from Longton in Staffordshire. Martha and Robert would eventually set up a small ironmongery business at Brithweunydd Road in Trealaw but their business closed when they relocated to Porthcawl during the 1920s.

While James and Gwen would have been excited at the prospect of starting a small business, they could not have envisaged the difficulties ahead in the few years before the First World War.

At 3.45pm on Friday 11th March in 1910 the abandoned "Gwennies", a disused coal level on the hillside above Clydach Vale filled with water and burst its banks. It created havoc, sending water rushing down Adam Street and Wern Street, just above Court Street. It swept into the local junior school, carrying some of the children into the yard where the surrounding high stone wall served to dam up the water. While the headmaster and staff succeeded in rescuing many of the children, three unfortunately drowned in the school yard, and a woman and a six-month-old baby also died in an adjacent street.

Some houses were demolished in the torrent and others simply flooded. Mabel Bevan, a neighbour of James and Gwen, worked as an assistant at the school and was lucky to escape. The effect on the tight-knit community was traumatic and continued throughout the lengthy investigation which followed.

Adam Street, Clydach Vale, after the floods in 1910

As if that were not enough tragedy for one year, in October 1910 the 12,000 miners and others employed by mine owners Cambrian Combine went on strike. The conflict between the union and the company, which began over payment for working a difficult seam at Penygraig, escalated into a deeper rift. By the beginning of November the bitterness of this dispute had resulted in the famous disturbances at Tonypandy when 60 shops were damaged during riots which ensured the town's name became known everywhere for the wrong reasons. Some 1,500 police reinforcements were brought in from Cardiff, Swansea, Bristol and London plus soldiers from the Lancashire Fusiliers and the 218th Hussars, and two miners died in the fight for better wages and conditions.

Clydach Vale Democratic Club Distress Committee, 1910, helping to reduce the suffering of the families of miners involved in the Cambrian Strike

Skirmishes took place between the police and strikers who were attempting to stop blacklegs working at Glamorgan Colliery. In an encounter at Tonypandy Square on 7 November 1910 windows were broken and some shops looted.

All this was occurring as a backdrop to Gwen's second pregnancy and at a time when the Leekes were trying to establish their small business from the front room of their Tonypandy home; hardly the most auspicious time for their first son, Llewellyn David Norman Leeke, to arrive on 10th June 1911. Gwen must have thought back to life in Baglan and the peace of the Vale of Glamorgan and wondered where on earth her husband had brought her to live. James, too, must have had his doubts as he seriously considered emigrating with his family to Canada at this time.

But, despite the difficulties that were part and parcel of the mining area, this was a community where people helped one another and gave practical and emotional support at times when others needed it most. Grandmothers were likely to be around the corner in the next street, close by to help and be helped, and cousins, uncles and aunts were all likely to be within walking distance, consolidating that sense of community and support. Choirs, brass bands, dramatic societies, pigeon clubs, working men's clubs, miners' institutes, churches and chapels gave the area a spirit that would be good for any emerging local business. Within a few years the bustling mining industry was at the height of its prosperity, employing some 48,000 men.

Politically the Rhondda Valleys were a fertile breeding ground for the emerging Labour Party in those few years before the outbreak of the First World War. The inherent dangers and injustices within the mining industry forged a strong bond between workers and intellectuals. It would not be until after the war that the Labour Party became the major party of the left in British politics, but its campaigns in the mining valleys of South Wales would have won the support of many a small retailer: for up-and-coming businessmen like James Leeke the harsh economic reality was that injured, unemployed, dead or impoverished miners were not good for business.

When the country did go to war in 1914 the Rhondda mining industry made enormous contributions. Thousands of miners enlisted, while production output broke all records. Yet an air of militancy was never far away. The entire coalfield came out on strike in 1915 despite wartime anti-strike legislation – and succeeded in obtaining wage increases. By the end of the war in 1918 the Rhondda mining community was at the forefront of trade union activism in Britain.

James's natural sympathies prompted his strong interest in the early and turbulent years of the Labour Party in the Rhondda. The leader of the Labour Party and its first MP, Keir Hardie, allegedly supped at the Leekes' table during a Rhondda visit. James was an eloquent man and he often held sway at The Monkey Club: a man of forthright views, he was often referred to by his sister, Mart, as someone who *"should have been a Philadelphia lawyer"*. His socialist leanings and his standing amongst the miners had spared his shop window during the Tonypandy riots while those of his fellow shopkeepers were shattered during battles with troops and police.

An incident from the time of the Cambrian disputes illustrates James's sympathy for the miners' cause. The police used to charge down Court Street hill and confront the strikers in Tonypandy (Pandy) Square and anyone coming up the hill would be caught up. An old man who had become involved in this way ran through the Leekes' shop and out to the backyard where chasing police caught him and beat him unmercifully. They subsequently attempted to prosecute him and, before the case came to court, James was visited by Sgt. Letheren of Penygraig who was related to Gwen by marriage. He was warned that if he testified against the police he would never be safe from becoming a police target himself in the Rhondda Valley. He was not intimidated and did testify against the police and the old man escaped the charge.

Professionally James had neither the patience nor the desire to deal face-to-face with his customers. While his strength lay in wheeling and dealing, Gwen was well-suited to handling the penniless and irascible who ventured into the small ironmonger's shop, her time spent dealing with inebriated and sometimes querulous customers at The Three Horseshoes in Peterston standing her in good stead. The hours were long; 8am to 9pm Monday to Saturday, except Thursday afternoon. The bell on the shop would often ring several times during a meal and whoever was nearest the door would serve the customer, usually with paraffin. It was a partnership that prospered, despite James being a somewhat restless soul.

On 4th June 1917 James and Gwen completed their family with the birth of their third child, William James David, known as Bill. As South Wales emerged from the First World War years James Leeke's business had consolidated substantially. Well enough certainly for him to go back to Herefordshire on missions to prepare various property holdings in anticipation of his eventual return to his original home.

With considerable foresight, he began building up property holdings in the Golden Valley area of his native Herefordshire. In 1919 he bought the dilapidated Urishay Castle at Peterchurch from a bankrupt Swedish match manufacturer and renowned socialist for £300. He made a sizeable profit selling its oak panelling to an agent for the McAlpine family who then sold it in the United States. This was to provide capital to assist in the later purchase of land nearby at Kerrys Gate in 1925 and the building of two houses and four bungalows in the early Thirties. An additional bungalow was built at Hazeldene, and Longwood Farm was leased from its Caerphilly-based owner.

Urishay Castle pictured in 1980

30

In the meantime, their middle child Llewellyn, always affectionately known as Llew, had moved up to Blaenclydach Junior School on 28th August 1918 after a period spent in the Infant School. The post-war log books for many Rhondda schools show that the curricula contained topics that would seem somewhat quaint by today's standards. Llew's health and moral tuition would include such exciting topics as *"the process of digestion in mouth, stomach and intestines"*, *"intemperance and drinking"*, *"tobacco – its evil effects"* and *"good and bad personal habits"*.

Unfortunately, the strong influence of the chapels on educational welfare could not prevent the endless health problems which made school in the Rhondda in the post war years a seemingly dangerous place to be. High absenteeism was most often due to colds, mumps, measles, whooping cough, chicken pox and scarlet fever. Hundreds of people, including children, died from the worldwide Spanish Flu epidemic in the year Llewellyn started primary school.

Homelife would have provided Llewellyn with an exciting if modest commercial environment. Shops in the Rhondda in the 20s and 30s had a particular style and culture accurately reflected by Gwyn Thomas, one of the Rhondda's best-known humorists and writers:

> *"The shops . . . in their bulging comprehensiveness, were a special feature of the Rhondda. They always reminded me of the stores in an American frontier town. Community centres in miniature, higgledy-piggledy piles of treasure in which the restless young found it easy to get lodged and lost. A half-hour before closing time a thorough sweep-through was made for missing persons.*

> *"Shoplifting in the less Calvinistic districts must have been something of an art form and several of the more distraught traders put the departing customers on the scales and charged them, not on individual items but on their total weight.*

*"In the lean years many shopkeepers showed an heroic comradeship with their needy customers and went irretrievably through the hoop because of it. The place was full of an oxygen of sharing and caring. If all the lights of the world were put out you could still see the Rhondda glow bright and consoling in the dark.*

*"The chip shops and Italian cafes were the heart of our night life. In my local chip shop I was hoisted nightly on to a lemonade box and made to sing for the waiting customers. As a reward I was fed with endless bags of "scrumps", fragments of batter made to smart with salt and swim in vinegar. My family had to rescue me when I showed signs of a chipped larynx and advanced carbohydrate poisoning, batter-fatigue."*

*[Gwyn Thomas]*

The Court Street household was bustling and busy with little separation between business and family life and regular reminders of life outside the four walls, as Arnold Letheren, the son of one of Gwen's sisters, recalls:

*"I remember staying, as a child, with Llewellyn at Court Street. It was an extremely crowded house. I used to sleep with Llew and his brother Bill and always ended up in the middle. I remember hearing this terrible clattering. I thought it was a pack of horses, but it was just the miners' night shift running home.*

*"Meals at Court Street were always great fun. There were continuous knocks on the front door with customers asking for some urgent item or other. Every meal was interrupted. I remember that Bill would frequently have to draw off paraffin for some customers. We joked that he would usually wash his hands five or six times during each meal to get rid of the smell of paraffin."*

*[Arnold Letheren]*

32

Roy Davies, one year older than Llew and so now well into his nineties, first became his close friend at school. He recalls that the family did not socialise much, spending their time working hard in the business. His memories include James Leeke working in the garage at the back of 178 Court Street, shodding pit ponies while his wife Gwen worked in the shop.

Although Llewellyn would no doubt have been working as an errand boy before he joined his father's business, it was in 1925, after leaving school at the age of 14, that he became fully employed by his father. Roy Davies remembers him starting the builders yard in 1927 at the back of the Monkey Club in Court Street by building a shack on land that was formerly a tip.

If times had been tough in the earlier years, then they were about to become much tougher. In those two decades between the two World Wars the great army of people who had poured into the Rhondda Valley from every part of Britain began slipping away. Pits began closing, in the words of Gwyn Thomas, *"like flies' eyes"* and, while the economy that had been buoyed up by coal began to crumble, the general, worldwide economic situation would shortly lurch into the years of the Great Depression.

By 1925 the post-war coal boom was over and the dark clouds of economic depression were moving in. Rhondda coal – the world's finest steam coal – was being supplanted by oil in both merchant and naval ships. This, combined with the seven-month coal strike of 1926 and the worldwide depression, gave the Rhondda one of Britain's highest unemployment rates and led to a huge outflow of population during the late 1920s and throughout the 1930s.

The decline of the coal industry in the 1920s in South Wales, and particularly the Rhondda area, hit the smaller coal companies. In 1925 the owners of Britain's coalfields asked their miners to accept cuts in wages and an extra hour on their working day. The miners' response summed up in their well-known slogan *"Not an hour on the day. Not a penny off the pay"* inevitably led to the events of 30th April 1926 when the mine-owners locked out all those who refused to accept their proposals. The British coalfield came to a stop.

With the support of the Trade Unions Congress (TUC) the General Strike was called on 3rd May 1926. Although the TUC called off the strike after nine days the South Wales miners fought on until the end of the year when starvation drove them back to work, defeated.

For Llewellyn it was a harsh introduction to the tough world of business. The priority in the late 1920s and early 1930s was survival. In 1932 over half the population of the Rhondda was registered as unemployed and unemployment benefit for a man, his wife and three children was about 20 shillings a week, which then reduced the longer he was out of work. So Llewellyn and his parents would have been running a business where people had great difficulty in paying. Self-service soup kitchens and disaster funds were the order of the day, broken up occasionally by the drama of a hunger march which usually underlined the frustration and futility of it all.

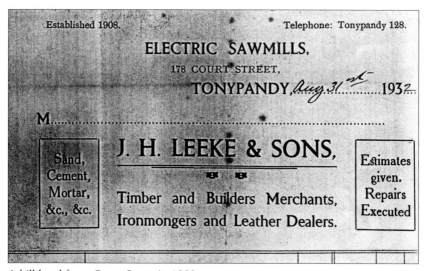

A bill head from Court Street in 1932

But despite the fact that almost a third of the Rhondda's population began leaving during these years, and that for those who remained it was a period of enormous mass unemployment, the Leekes' business survived intact, and Llewellyn took over the business completely from his father in 1933 at the age of 22. James was now able to take advantage of the apparently far more attractive business opportunities that were emerging away from the commercial turmoil of the Rhondda Valleys. Meanwhile Llewellyn Leeke added to his business activities and sourced extra work which would also provide jobs for his local community, using the lorry he had acquired for the business.

*"I remember Llewellyn in the early 1930s when I suppose I must have been ten or eleven years of age. Even then he was involved in supplying sub-contract labour to help work on the extension of the brewery at Pontyclun. He would get up early, drive the men to Pontyclun in the lorry and then return to carry on with his main business. Llew's brother Bill and I would often join them on the back of the lorry."*

*[Arnold Letheren]*

Llew's hard work was paying off and it was at this time he bought his first car – a black Austin 6. Buying the car was quite an occasion as it was the only one owned in the street. It was garaged at the rear of 178 Court Street in the building originally used by James when he was working as a blacksmith.

By 1933 James knew that, despite the difficulties of the depression years, Llewellyn was more than adept at running the business. He therefore decided to return to his home county of Herefordshire after over 25 years in South Wales. He and Gwen set up home at Oakdene Court, Kerrys Gate, near Abbey Dore, but his continuing close interest in Llewellyn's progress and almost daily contact are remembered by Arnold Letheren:

*"I remember at Court Street that the telephone would be 'red hot' in the evenings. This was because Jim would be*

Oakdene Court pictured in 2004

*'phoning from Herefordshire to check with Llewellyn how business had been each day. He always seemed interested in everything."*
                                                                    *[Arnold Letheren]*

Back in Herefordshire James was free to pursue his various other interests. He would sell the countless eggs his chickens provided and even supplied the local Woolworth's with tomato plants. His engineering skills were not forgotten and he supervised the building of a windmill at Oakdene to pump water from the nearby reservoir up to his house. Arthur Letheren, Gwen's brother-in-law, was a bricklayer who led the project:

*"I remember going to Oakdene in the early Thirties with Llewellyn. Sometimes there would be as many as 14 of us in two or three cars. We would sleep anywhere. Having a bath was always a risk if the windmill was not working – because of the clay soil you could emerge a bright red colour from head to foot!"*
                                            *[Arnold Letheren, Arthur's son]*

## Chapter 2

# THE NEXT GENERATION

James and Gwen's first-born, Doris Gwendoline Mary (1909-1985), went on to marry Oliver Davies, a grocer from Trealaw, Rhondda, in August 1940. They had two children, Clive (who undertook much of the research for this early part of the story) in 1941, and Margaret in 1945. James and Gwen's youngest child Bill grew up to marry Doris Griffiths, the eldest daughter of a farmer from Senghenydd, near Caerphilly, and moved initially to join his father at Longwood Farm near Kerrys Gate and then to Manor Farm at Longdon in Worcestershire. They had four children between 1940 and 1954 – Gwendoline, Richard, Andrew and Rosemary.

The wedding of Doris Leeke and Oliver Davies at Bacton Church, Hereford, in 1940. From the left, Ivor Davies, best man and brother to the groom, bridegroom Oliver, bride Doris, Betty Simon, bridesmaid, and James Leeke

While Bill joined his father, Doris still lived at 178 Court Street, teaching at Cwmclydach Junior Girls School, a post she had taken up in 1930. Later, after her husband Oliver had completed his training as an Anglican Minister in 1952, they would move to Worcestershire where they remained for the rest of their lives.

In the early Thirties Llewellyn was courting his future wife, Anne Maria (Myra) Jones. He had met her at a local hockey club function through his close, childhood friend Roy Davies who was later to be best man at their wedding.

The Cambrian Mixed Hockey Team 1933-1934 season: Llew Leeke can be seen in the back row, second from the right. Roy Davies, captain, is in the centre

Myra was the only child of David and Elizabeth Anne Jones. Myra's father had moved from Cardigan to the Rhondda at a time when work and the business prospects there would have seemed much more appealing than the agricultural world he left behind. Although also trained as a cooper (a maker of barrels for brewers), he was a born entrepreneur who eventually developed businesses as a builder, a wheelwright and an undertaker. He even obtained the dealership for Britannic motorcycles and sidecars, prestigious possessions during the early and mid 1920s. The coach-built sidecars alone sold for £18 and ten shillings in 1925 – a princely sum in a mining community and undoubtedly a classy product for a former farmhand to be selling. Following their marriage David and Elizabeth – who was a noted singer in the various chapels around Treorchy – settled in Bute Street in Treherbert. Myra was born on 14th June 1913 and went to the local school.

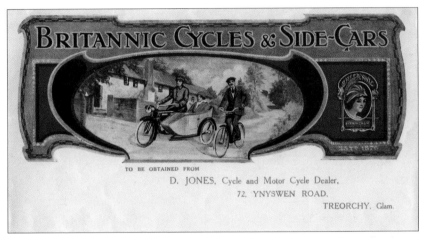

A letterhead from David Jones's business showing Britannic Cycles and Sidecars (early 1930s)

Llew and Myra's wedding on 25th October 1935 at Carmel Chapel in Treherbert was quite a society event, extensively reported in *The Rhondda Leader* and other local newspapers. Press reports referred to the fact that the bride was well-known in the local community as a prominent member of Carmel Chapel and as one of the organisers of the local Young People's Society.

Best man Roy Davies says that Llew and Myra had very different upbringings and Myra was concerned that Roy would lead her husband astray: Llew and his family never went to church and enjoyed the occasional drink while Myra and her parents were strong chapel-goers and strict teetotallers.

Llew and Myra's wedding in 1935. James Leeke stands behind the bridal couple with David Jones to his left and Roy Davies to his right. Gwen is seated on the right and Elizabeth Anne on the left

Following a large reception, the bride and groom left for their honeymoon in Torquay. They then returned to their first marital home back at Court Street in Tonypandy where they would live and develop the business until 1949.

As the Rhondda struggled through the later years of the Depression in the period up to 1940, Llewellyn extended his business through the Court Street shop and his builders yard with new suppliers and new products. Although the essence of the ironmongery trade remained the same as it had been in the previous decade, the business would now offer a more extensive range of household products. Pot-menders, washboards, "black pat" (beetle) traps and chamois leathers would be more profitable than miners' items such as patent pick handles and curling boxes.

It was during this time that Llew and Myra started their family with the birth of David on 11th October 1936. To embark upon family life and have grown a small family business during the 1930s and the run-up to the Second World War was no mean achievement.

Doris, Llew's sister, with Llew and Myra's first-born, David, at 178 Court Street in 1937. The Union Jack and crown seen in the window mark the coronation of King George VI. The bucket beside the pavement contained rubbish for collection, often knocked over by sheep wandering down from the mountain looking for food

Significant national and local events were happening around the young Leeke family at this time, not least the coronation of King George VI in 1937. On 30th August that same year local hero Tommy Farr, who also lived in Court Street, fought Joe Louis for the heavyweight championship of the world at the Yankee Stadium, New York in front of a crowd of 36,000. Tommy Farr, known as 'The Tonypandy Terror', was three years younger than Llew and had had his first fight over six rounds at the age of 12.

The fight with Joe Louis took place at 3am Rhondda time. The excitement in South Wales – particularly in Tonypandy – reached fever pitch as thousands of locals listened to the live broadcast. Joe Louis was known as the "Brown Bomber" because of his heavy punching which normally resulted in early knockouts, but the commentators reported he was behind on points as the fight neared the end. It was therefore a bitter disappointment when Louis was declared the winner. Although he had lost the fight, Tommy Farr had won the respect of the world and earned a place in boxing history.

Looking up Court Street from the Leekes' shop on the day neighbour Tommy Farr returned home after his epic fight against world champion Joe Louis in 1937

Another famous resident of Tonypandy, born in 1909, was George Thomas, Viscount Tonypandy, who was long known to the Leeke family and had been at Tonypandy Secondary Grammar School at the same time as Llew's sister Doris:

> *"When I met him on a tour of the Houses of Parliament some years ago I had a great welcome and we had a long chat about the old times in Tonypandy. He seemed very pleased to introduce me to a number of his colleagues as a native of his home town. He really was very proud of his roots and upbringing."*
>
> *[David Leeke]*

David Leeke's childhood memories of the shop are few but vivid, and those of his playmate and Court Street next-door neighbour Norman Tudball *"quite magical"*:

> *"I have a clear memory of the huge sheets of leather which used to hang there, used by miners for shoe repairs. There were all sorts of miners' provisions, picks and shovels, zinc baths and, of course, miners' 'snap' [lunch] boxes. In addition nails, screws, all types of fittings, pots, pans and lamps were sold. Garden tools, fireguards, bakestones and oil and paraffin could be bought over the counter."*
>
> *[David Leeke]*

> *"I remember that the shop in Court Street was like an Aladdin's Cave. They seemed to have everything there. It must have taken them ages to organise it into some shape. It was certainly a great place to play for young boys."*
>
> *[Norman Tudball]*

While chapels could still raise some passion for the religious festivals at Easter and Whitsun, the interest in the new cinemas and jazz and band music brought some escapism from the old

Eisteddfodic culture of the valleys. Some chinks of economic relief became evident with a range of new manufacturing industries brought into the lower coalfield areas such as Treforest near Pontypridd through Government-supported schemes; yet that relief was to be short-lived.

All this would soon change dramatically with the outbreak of the Second World War, which brought an upturn in local economic activity. The wartime need for power ensured coal mining received a new impetus and many former miners were released from the Forces to return to the pits. But for Myra it must have seemed that history was repeating itself: by now, like Gwen a quarter of a century earlier, she had a three-year-old child and a business to keep going at the outset of a World War.

James and Gwen Leeke, with Llew and Myra and James's first grandchild, David, at Oakdene Court in 1940

Llewellyn continued his business expansion plans and in 1939 he moved his builders yard from the tip behind the Monkey Club in Court Street where he had started it, to a larger building at Brynamlog next to the King George's playing field and park. He was also widely active in supporting the war effort at home, as Arnold Letheren recalls:

*"I remember Llewellyn so well during the war years. He was such a hard-working character. Because he had his own transport, he was involved in storing timber for the Ministry of Defence. He would collect this from Robinson & David, the importers, at Cardiff Docks and take this either to his new yard at Clydach or to a special store at Oakdene Court in Hereford. Apart from this, he was involved in collecting and delivering milk and even had time to work as a special constable."*

[Arnold Letheren]

The Special Constabulary where Llew served during the Second World War. (Llew is in the middle row, fifth from the left)

But Court Street was not just the business premises, it was also the family home – and the family was growing with the births there of Gerald on 29th August 1941 and Diane on 9th August 1943. For the three young children growing up wartime was a part of everyday life. Very few people had vehicles in those days, so the only ones regularly seen were the single-decker buses

– painted grey to avoid being spotted from the air – which went up Thomas Street and down Court Street on a service to the top of Clydach Vale. Regular school air-raid warnings would see children leaving lessons to gather in the concrete buildings in the yard, which were specially built for such emergencies.

At the end of their shifts troops of blackened faces would pass the shop on their way home from the two Clydach Vale collieries, the Cambrian and Gorki. Eldest son David recalls going into Norman Tudball's house next door and seeing his father, a miner, bathing in a galvanised tub in front of the open fire in the living room.

David Leeke remembers family life in Court Street well:

Norman Tudball with David and Gerald near the railway line behind Court Street in 1945

*"I remember playing with nails in the shop and serving paraffin from the tank behind the counter. There was a small office behind the shop with an old-fashioned telephone. It had an earpiece separate from the speaker.*

*"The remaining rooms downstairs were a living room and a kitchen. The kitchen overlooked the back yard, which was on a higher level. It was quite small and had a table, chairs, sink unit, cooker and fridge, and a cupboard to store all the pots and pans where we often found what we called 'black pats' crawling around.*

*"At the rear there was a garage where the Austin 6 was kept and a built-on greenhouse where tomatoes were grown. There was also a separate coal shed and the dog kennel where our cocker spaniel was housed.*

*"Upstairs we had a front room over the shop with a double bed where Gerald and I slept. Diane used the single room, which had a window overlooking the back garden. Behind this was a larger bedroom, with a bathroom attached, where Mother and Father slept. Access to the only toilet in the house was through our parents' bedroom. I suppose we were extremely fortunate to have a bathroom and toilet indoors, because almost all the other houses in the street had no such facilities, only a toilet at the bottom of the back garden."*

[David Leeke]

(Left to right) Gerald, Diane and David in 1946

For the growing Leeke family home life and business were equally family affairs, with Myra's nearby relatives playing their part in both:

Diane and a friend in Court Street after the blizzards in 1947

*"My grandmother from Treherbert was a frequent visitor, helping Mother with her three children, as she also looked after the shop. Father was working in the yard with*

*my maternal grandfather and Clarence, our lorry driver, who drove the large lorry to pick up sand from Cardiff on a regular basis and also coke and lime, which were used to make mortar used as a cheaper alternative to sand and cement. He also made deliveries of the larger orders. Father also delivered orders for building materials, grates, timber, toilet pans etc throughout the Rhondda Valleys in our pick-up truck.*

*"My grandfather used to make wooden toys for us. I can remember a scooter with wooden wheels, which needed replacing frequently, as there were not many toys around at that time and it was used a great deal by me and my friends.*

*"Thursday was half-day closing day in the Rhondda and Father always went to the warehouses in Cardiff to pick up various goods for resale in the shop. Occasionally Mother took us on the bus to Treherbert to visit her mother and other relatives who lived nearby.*

*"On our return we would get off the bus at the square in Tonypandy and walk up the steep hill for about ¼ mile to our house. One day Mother was carrying Diane, and Gerald and I were walking, when Gerald fainted. Luckily for Mother the district nurse was walking behind us and carried Gerald home before bringing him round.*

*"In those days Sunday was very different from today. No shops were open and we used to go to church regularly three times, for Morning Service, for afternoon Sunday School and then for Evensong. I think I joined the choir when I was six and remained a chorister until I went away to school. If it was a nice day we would take a trip in the afternoon to Kenfig Pool as the seaside was out-of-bounds during the war."*

[David Leeke]

*"I do remember Llewellyn's father-in-law, David Jones, the carpenter who used to look after the yard. I seem to remember that he worked until he was well into his eighties.*

48

*He always liked to talk to people in Welsh. He was a very tall chap with glasses and always wore a trilby hat."*

*[family friend Elvet Williams]*

Meanwhile, at Oakdene Court, James was still interested in property investment. In 1941, he persuaded Llew to purchase Manor Farm, Longdon, near Tewkesbury, and to lease it to his younger brother Bill, who was farming at Longwood Farm close to his parents' home.

In the meantime James had decided to sell his property at Oakdene Court and build a new home near to son Bill on the farm at Longdon. He named it Baglan House after his wife's birthplace but shortly before it was completed he died from heart failure in September 1942 aged 62.

*"I remember my father telling me about the day my grandfather died. Father was travelling to Longdon in the car when it broke down and failed to restart. Being wartime the only option was to hitch a lift – which was not easy with few vehicles on the road. He eventually arrived there many hours later by walking several miles to complete the journey."*

*[David Leeke]*

Baglan House gave the Rhondda-based family a much-enjoyed weekend retreat which David Leeke remembers well:

*"So from then on we had a regular routine for bank holidays, except Christmas. The business would close on Saturday evening and re-open the following Wednesday. After closing on Saturday we would drive to Longdon, a drive which today takes 75 minutes, but in those days took three hours as there were no motorways or dual carriageways. We would drive through towns such as Pontypridd, Ystrad Mynach, Pontypool, Raglan, Monmouth, Ross and Ledbury. We usually arrived in time for Father to pop down to the local pub before closing time with his brother Bill.*

*"We still had the Austin 6 which was used for our trips to Longdon. Like most cars at the time it was not unusual for it to be difficult to start or to break down. I can remember the car not starting, and then we would use the starting handle at the front of the bonnet.*

*"They were very happy times and great family occasions as Father's sister Doris and her family would also be there, as well as his brother Bill and family. I remember persuading Uncle Bill to play cricket on the lawn in front of the farmhouse and he always made sure all the other boys in the family joined in. As I was the oldest grandchild and the keenest to play, he always made sure I was out lbw if I was hit on the leg.*

*"The farm today is arable with no livestock but, in those days, cows, sheep and chickens were kept. I spent many happy holidays milking the cows, feeding the chickens and collecting the eggs they had laid."*

[David Leeke]

Clive Davies also remembers the holidays – and Gwen, his grandmother – well:

*"She had a wonderful nature. Never saw her angry, she sang hymns endlessly, loved the fresh air and had the windows open and curtains billowing winter or summer. But she was a diabolical cook! Many of her breakfasts were whipped by all of us off the plate into a newspaper and down the disused well in her front garden. She could turn an egg into black mush in the blink of an eye!"*

[Clive Davies]

Gwen died aged 86 in July 1967 at her daughter Doris's home at Broadwas, Worcestershire. Both James and Gwen Leeke lie in Longdon churchyard.

*Chapter 3*

# THE DUNRAVEN STREET YEARS

Life in post-war South Wales – and especially the Rhondda Valleys – was very different from the dark days of the 1930s recession; in 1945 expectations in Wales were high. The Labour Government elected in that year was massively endorsed by the Welsh electorate – of the 36 constituencies in Wales 25 had been won by Labour. The creation of the National Health Service and the general strengthening of the welfare state were particularly welcomed in Wales and the social improvements were also good news for businesses.

The Government would gradually carry out a far-reaching programme of bringing industries and services under state control and ownership. In the Rhondda Valleys the nationalis-ation of the coal industry – still the major source of local employment in 1947 – was particularly warmly welcomed although, by then, many of the collieries in that area were in a perilous state.

The inevitable pit closures had a great effect on employment levels, alleviated only by the fact that many people were now travelling to work outside the Rhondda in the new industries established at the edges of the coalfields, typically on the large industrial estates at Hirwaun, Bridgend and Treforest.

But, while the population of the Rhondda was declining from the late Forties onwards, the number of owner-occupied houses was rising. Although few new houses had been built in the Rhondda since 1914, affordable but poor quality accommodation was still available, and the dwindling population was keen to buy and renovate their own homes. Labour's post-war policy of upgrading housing stock and the extensive use of pre-fabricated homes both helped create an air of optimism.

This was the climate that spawned a growing home improvement market and Llewellyn Leeke was in at the beginning, determined that his family would not again see such difficult times as he had:

> "My parents both worked extremely hard throughout their lives. They both started working in the late 1920s when times were very hard and this continued in the 1930s and 1940s. My father gave Mother a limited amount to live on and she did an extremely good job, making sure her children were well looked after often at the expense of herself. I remember her buying various vitamins to supplement our diet and Scotts Emulsion was always a great favourite, especially during the winter.

> "After experiencing such difficult times Father was determined to build up some capital in case those times returned, and to ensure that his children did not have to experience the hardship he had in the pre-war period."
>
> [David Leeke]

Although he remained involved with the Glamorgan Police Force as a special constable, after the war Llewellyn returned to concentrating fully on his own business and decided it was time to expand. He started to build up capital in the 1940s and, in 1948, bought a larger shop in poor condition in Dunraven Street, Tonypandy – which would later become one of the Rhondda's main shopping areas. Shortly after its purchase the family closed the Court Street shop and moved to a new home, Mountview, on Llantrisant Road in Groesfaen, near Llantrisant, in December 1949. Llewellyn had bought both the Dunraven Street shop and the house without having to borrow any money:

> "The Dunraven Street shop was a big step forward, going from a one-roomed shop in Court Street to one many times the size in Tonypandy's main street. As it was only a few

*years after the war, all types of materials were difficult to obtain. Father and Clarence, his driver, would drive to the Midlands every few weeks with the big lorry and visit various suppliers to see what was available. They would always arrive home with the lorry full of goods such as fireplaces, Foresight cookers, toilet pans and seats, sinks, gutters and downpipes, frets and fires, brickbacks etc. These would enable Father to gradually fill the new shop with goods and materials."*

*[David Leeke]*

Dunraven Street in 1908

Supported by the family's builders yard at Brynamlog, the Dunraven Street shop would be the base of the business for the next 18 years. According to first son David, it was a family affair from day one:

*"The Dunraven Street shop opened during one of my summer holidays from Hereford Cathedral School. My father arranged for me to stand outside the shop and try and encourage people to come in and have a look around.*

*What I remember most are rows of tiled fireplaces which were stacked up all along one wall. We sold some bathrooms to begin with, but these were not too popular at the time as people were used to using tin baths in front of their kitchen fires.*

"Every school holiday I was expected to help out working in the shop, leaving the house at Groesfaen with Father at 7.45am every morning and returning with him by 6.30pm in the evening. I was allowed a day off occasionally to watch Glamorgan play cricket at Cardiff Arms Park.

"We had no heating in the shop, so my first job was to light the fire in the office. Father would leave me to look after the shop while he attended the yard and delivered orders. Mother would come up on the bus by 11 o'clock three or four days a week, and Father would return on the other days to catch up with the paperwork and help out serving the customers if we were busy. If the family went on holiday, my grandmother would come along and help me run the business.

"If Mother was not in the shop, it was my duty to sort out lunch and I would go to various local grocers and fruiterers to buy the ingredients. It usually consisted of salad with ham and a small pudding."

[David Leeke]

This typical valleys ironmonger and builders merchant was operated almost entirely by the family – but the local business community was also strong and supportive:

"The business people around us were all friends. Billy 'Butch' Davies, the butcher, had the shop next door and used to call in to see if I was okay. Next to him was Gwynfor Jones, the newsagent whom I visited each morning to buy The Western Mail. Next door to them was another butcher and then

*Lloyds Bank where I would go when Father arrived to bank the takings and obtain change for the till. Next door the other side was Mrs Tweezle (china shop), then Ed Moyle, the barber who cut our hair, and Don Taylor – Mother's preferred grocer as he always had very tasty ham. There were also Tony Servini (coffee shop) and Bill Jones and his cousin J D Jones (fruiterers). It was a real community."*

*[David Leeke]*

JD Jones in his apron stands outside his fish, fruit and vegetable shop in Dunraven Street in 1936

These close local relationships played an important part in Llewellyn's business practices:

*"He would let people have credit purely on his understanding of them and knowledge of the local community. Sometimes you couldn't understand how he would agree to credit but nobody ever let my father down."*

*[David Leeke]*

The Dunraven Street premises were long and narrow with no heating except for the coal fire in the office. Access was poor to the basement which was used as a tile store – an important part of the business throughout the Fifties.

Following the long period of austerity demand for tiling in the home seemed insatiable. By the mid-Fifties the tiling industry, particularly in the Staffordshire area, had become increasingly mechanised, costs reduced and the range of colours and designs extended. The main British manufacturers, Johnsons and Pilkingtons, sold the large quantities of slightly sub-standard tiles produced through mechanisation at a fraction of the price of the first-grade ones through a clearing house in Stoke-on-Trent. On his buying trips Llewellyn would purchase thousands of yards of good quality seconds to sell at Dunraven Street at attractive prices; demand increased dramatically after a regular series of advertisements in *The Western Mail* drew people from all over South Wales. As David Leeke recalls, his father had a strategy to ensure he got the best price:

> *"It seemed as though people were tiling half of South Wales in the 1950s. I used to go with Father occasionally on these regular trips to the clearing house. We would arrive at about midday and check the prices of various tiles with the clearing house manager, a man called Dennis. We would then wine and dine him at lunch and usually agree a lower price when we returned afterwards. Many years later, after Father's death, Dennis paid us a visit and explained that he was wise to Father's tactics and always added an amount to the original price as he knew he would be knocked down after lunch."*
>
> *[David Leeke]*

Through the 1950s more and more local councils and private homeowners began concentrating on home improvements, extensions and house-building. It was a good time to be a builders merchant as people were embracing property improvement and local authorities were providing home improvement grants. In homes carpets were replacing linoleum, and road travel increased as even manual workers could afford to own their own car. The extensive growth in television ownership throughout those years typified the cultural and economic changes.

> *"We used to sell hundreds of toilet pans to the local council and to private householders. They would be seconds from Johnsons and always white. It was as though there was a campaign during the 1950s to replace all the toilets in the Rhondda."*
>
> *[David Leeke]*

A few bathrooms and, later, some basic kitchen units were on display at Dunraven Street, but it was fireplaces which occupied the majority of the floor space and Llewellyn's lorry livery proclaimed *"We Are Grate People"*:

The tailgate and number plate of the delivery truck

A Leekes advertisment in the
Rhondda Leader, 1951

RHONDDA GRATE SPECIALIST

The above EAGLE GRATE with Slate
Mantel, Tiled Hearth and Curb
£11 10s. 0d.
FREE OF PURCHASE TAX.
Also 50 Tiled Grates in Stock.
Prices £3 to £20.

**J. H. LEEKE**
AND SONS
**TONYPANDY.**
Tel. Tonypandy 128.

*"The shop was about 12 to 15 feet wide but at least 60 feet long. The office was about 40 feet back and there were tiled fireplaces stacked all along the length of one wall, as well as about three in the window. We usually sold 15 to 20 fireplaces in an average week, at least half of them on a Saturday.*

*"On another wall were cookers, the most popular being the Foresight cooker. During the early 1950s the all-night burner, which controlled the amount of coal used, was introduced and this became a very popular seller.*

*"We also started to sell bathrooms and kitchen units from Jenmore in Gilfach and these were on display. Above the wall displays we had shelves on which were stocked all types of paint and associated materials.*

*"The counter, where the till and weighing scales were situated, was about halfway down the shop. In those days nothing was pre-packed so we weighed most items, such as cement, plaster, sand and nails of various sorts and sizes."*

*[David Leeke]*

Llewellyn knew what his local customers wanted and, while he offered them the more modern products which were coming onto the market, he didn't forget the basics that proved enduringly popular:

*"We also sold all sorts of ironmongery and things like colliers' tins, water cans and so on. Every December my father used to buy hundreds of turkey cooking tins from Cardiff. These were all sizes and we used to pull his leg saying that he would be left with huge amounts of stock. I don't know how he did it but it seemed every year every one of the turkey tins would be sold."*

*[David Leeke]*

In this optimistic climate competition was to be expected, but Dunraven Street's central location, coupled with Llewellyn's drive and energy, proved key to commercial success, as family friends testify:

> *"There was another shop in Tonypandy, Jones the Ironmongers, which was a larger shop. I think there was also another one at the bottom end of Tonypandy. However, all the locals would go to Leekes for convenience."*
>
> [Norman Tudball]

> *"The Dunraven Street store was extremely busy, particularly at weekends. I remember that Llewellyn was very much a hands-on manager. He would be moving fireplaces, delivering tiles or timber but keeping an eye on everything. On his so-called days off he would make buying trips into Cardiff."*
>
> [Elvet Williams]

Meanwhile the family was growing up – and growing! While David was away at school in Hereford, Gerald and Diane had joined junior schools at Miskin and Pontyclun when the family moved to Groesfaen in 1949. Youngest brother Stuart was born on 9th March 1950 and, in September 1953, Gerald started at Cowbridge Grammar School with Diane starting at St James's College, Malvern two years later.

Llewellyn's belief in the future retail boom extended to his investment of the company profits: from the early 1950s he began to purchase shares in companies like Marks & Spencer and Woolworths. He also invested money in loans with various local authorities including the Rhondda Borough Council, which earned a good rate of interest.

Financial awareness was obviously a family trait as eldest son David, on leaving school in 1955, joined RH March & Son in Cardiff, a large and prestigious firm of chartered accountants, to commence his five-year articles. Still working in the business every Saturday morning, helping his father with the accounts and completing the PAYE for employees, he qualified as a chartered accountant in 1960.

In that same year second son Gerald joined RH March to complete his five-year articles. Although, like the whole family, he had been involved in the business right from his schooldays, now for the first time he was free to help on those busy Saturday mornings. While at school his Saturdays had been spent playing rugby and cricket, playing for Cowbridge Grammar School in the mornings and, depending on the season, for Pontyclun at rugby and Miskin Manor at cricket alongside brother David in the afternoons. A keen and talented sportsman who represented Wales at both sports, his rugby career was cut short by shoulder injuries.

Gerald as captain of Cowbridge Grammar School's rugby team in the late 1950s (centre, with ball)

On 25th October 1960 Llew and Myra celebrated their silver wedding anniversary with a dinner party at the Royal Hotel in Cardiff. It was their first big family celebration and was enjoyed by over 50 guests including Llew's mother, Myra's parents, cousins, close friends and Llew's brother and sister with their families.

Llew and Myra cut the cake at their Silver Wedding party

Llew's mother Gwen and Myra's parents with seven of Gwen's grand-children

Through the early 1960s David continued to work in the shop on Saturday mornings, while Gerald was in the yard helping with deliveries and orders which came in thick and fast – and Llewellyn would never refuse an order on a Saturday for same-day delivery.

Soon after qualifying as a chartered accountant David was to put his long experience of working in the business to the test when, in early 1961, Llew was rushed into hospital. David was given leave from his employer RH March to run the business supported by his mother Myra and sister Diane, who by now was working full-time in the company after completing a secretarial course in London. Llew was anxious to resume work but it was eight months before he had completely recovered and David was able to return to his own job.

In 1962 Diane married Alan Cook who, himself, joined the business in 1964 and remembers the early days fondly:

*"Coming down from the north of England I didn't know much about the South Wales valleys. I clearly remember*

Oak Street in Clydach Vale and couldn't understand why everyone washed the pavement in front of their house. I remember Llewellyn explaining to me that Oak Street had the reputation of being the cleanest street in the valleys. I'm not sure if it's still like that now.

"Coming from Grimsby I had a great problem with pronunciation. I remember asking one day how to get to Lionel-a-Pia (Llwynypia).

"I can remember that we worked very hard in the yard. One Saturday at about 11.45am a local company, JJ Plating, rang up and asked for 10 tons of sand to be delivered immediately. We never let a customer down and four of us began loading it by hand. I remember David complaining that he had to leave for cricket but the four of us got stuck in. We must have moved 1200 shovelfuls of sand between four of us to ensure delivery.

"Llewellyn always looked the part of an ironmonger. He would wear an old trilby hat and a grey shopcoat with no buttons, usually tied up with a bit of string around the middle. He smartened up considerably, of course, later on when we expanded.

"Although Llewellyn was excellent with people, he never liked dogs. I remember going to Cornwall Road in Williamstown with him to deliver two bags of cement and there was a great 'beware of the dog' sign on the garden gate. I opened the gate and Llewellyn followed behind. Immediately two Alsatian dogs appeared and I heard a thump and a bang behind me. The thump was Llewellyn dropping his bag of cement and the bang was the gate closing. Then the dogs almost licked me to death!"

[Alan Cook]

In June 1963 David Leeke joined Williams Ross in Pontypridd, the firm of accountants who had acted for his father since before the war. His professional links with J H Leeke & Sons strengthened when he became a partner at the firm in 1965 and took over responsibility for looking after the accounts of the family business, which had been trading as a limited company since 1956.

Despite its growth the administration of the business remained in many ways much the same as it had been before the war. To the bemusement of Llewellyn's two accountancy-qualified sons he would still take the shop takings to Lloyds Bank in Dunraven Street in his back pocket! Those takings would have been kept in his old open-drawer till – and there were no price lists; everything depended on Llewellyn's memory.

That style was to change when Gerald decided to join the family business in January 1966 after qualifying as a chartered accountant at RH March. Despite the firm's status – it would, years later, become part of internationally renowned accountants Deloitte & Touche – Gerald decided the life of an accountant was not for him and told his bosses he had other plans. One of the senior partners tried to counsel him not to make such a foolish move to a small family business with a modest turnover in an area like the Rhondda which was perceived as being in terminal decline.

1965 **YOU** 1965

Are invited to meet your old established Friends

**LEEKE'S**
**OF TONYPANDY**

again this year on their show stand No. 2 at
**THE RHONDDA TRADES FAIR**

We are known to you as 'GRATE' People
So be sure to visit our stand No. 2 and see our NEW and colourful designs in:—

**MODERN FIREPLACES    SINK UNITS**
**BATHROOM SUITES**

Also other General Household Commodities—including. . .

**TILES—for ceilings, walls and floors**

BRIGHTEN Your Homes with
BRIGHT Ideas fulfilled by
BRIGHT Purchases from our large stocks.

We cater for everyone at prices to suit their pockets.

YOU are also welcome to visit our showrooms at

**36 DUNRAVEN STREET, TONYPANDY**

Bus stops outside our door—ask for **LEEKE'S**

A Leekes advertisement taken from the 1965 Rhondda Traders Fair brochure

**SPECIAL BARGAINS**
DURING THE FINAL WEEK OF

**LEEKE'S CASH SALE**
SAMPLE OFFERS :
**GRATES from £4.19.6**
**Sink Units from £12.19.6**
**Bathroom Suites from £35**
INSULATION BOARD. 8 x 4. 13/11
CORRUGATED PERSPEX. Per Foot 3/-
GLAZED WALL TILES. Sq. Yd. 12/6
Also MARLEY FLOOR TILES, CEIILNG TILES, TIMBER, QUARRY TILES, Etc.
ALL LESS 2/- IN THE £
**36 DUNRAVEN STREET TONYPANDY**
Tel. 3228

A Leekes advertisement taken from the Rhondda Leader (1965)

Gerald's involvement in the business was now total and typically enthusiastic. While he felt that there was great potential to increase turnover and profits, he recognised the obvious weaknesses and barriers to growth in a business that gave generous credit and discounts to builders. He also recognised that competition among builders merchants in the Rhondda was significant, dominated by a few larger companies such as Pontypridd Builders Supplies, Paul's and British Dredging.

With Llewellyn's encouragement Gerald extended the range at Dunraven Street and established kitchen and bathroom displays on the upper floor. The house next door at number 37, previously a china shop, was taken over in the early 1960s and became an additional showroom. In 1965 the company turnover had reached £38,000, but the shop's limitations were obvious as the demand for home improvements to the Rhondda's housing stock was enormous. To compete and grow the business would need a larger premises and a strategy based on developing the DIY concept where, not only builders, but all customers could enjoy the benefits of self-selection and a wider choice for immediate payment. A start was made by increasing the DIY range and dealing directly with a larger number of manufacturers. Equally important to the successful growth of the business, Gerald began to introduce a more sophisticated accounting system.

For Llewellyn, running a successful family business meant both bringing new generations into the forefront of running the company *and* involving business in family life. When David Leeke married Jeanette Williams in 1966 the wedding was arranged for a Thursday at the request of his father, as it was half-day closing in the Rhondda. Except for Clarence, the lorry driver, only family members were employed in the business at that time, so it would have meant closing for the day and he was reluctant to do so on a Saturday, by far the busiest day of the week. The wedding took place on Thursday, 1st September 1966 at St Isan's Church, Llanishen, Cardiff, followed by a reception in Cardiff Castle. The couple had met when Jeanette joined David at accountants RH March in 1961 and her father, a captain in the Merchant Navy, was able to be home on leave for the wedding. They set up their family home in Ystradowen, near Cowbridge in the Vale of Glamorgan.

Their son Timothy was born at St David's Hospital, Cardiff in January 1972, followed by three daughters, Victoria in March 1974, Charlotte in October 1976 and Elizabeth in February 1978. All four children graduated from University, before going on to gain professional qualifications: Timothy and Elizabeth as chartered accountants, Victoria as an actuary and Charlotte a professional musician after obtaining a Masters in Music.

In this same year, for J H Leeke & Sons the issue of adequate premises was clearly a priority: the shop in Dunraven Street was structurally inadequate and had no space for car parking, and the builders yard at Brynamlog was too small and in a very poor location.

The old goods yard station at Trealaw, Rhondda became surplus to the Railway Board's requirements and came onto the market. Its position was excellent for deliveries to the two Rhondda Valleys and it was large enough to combine the retail premises and builders yard together with some car parking.

The station was eventually bought through auction by closed tender when Llewellyn's bid of £5,110 was accepted.

*Chapter 4*

# THE MOVE TO STATION YARD

As the Brynamlog Yard transferred to the new Station Yard in 1967, Clydach Vale's Cambrian pit closed along with many others as part of a general programme of colliery closures that had begun in 1955. There was an inevitable concern that the mass unemployment of the inter-war years would return to the Rhondda Valleys, which had been almost totally dependent on the coal industry. However, through the 1950s and 1960s, government policy had encouraged many new industries – such as engineering, manufacturing and car assembly – to establish in South Wales, bringing new jobs to the area.

These newer industries, along with the residual employment still provided in the traditional industries of coal, steel and tinplate, in fact ensured that reasonable employment levels had returned to South Wales by the mid-Sixties. The possibility of alternative employment probably explains why so many colliery closures were accepted by the miners.

Colliery closures and employment levels apart, the 1960s brought an explosive and unprecedented cultural and social change: the "Swinging Sixties" with their amazing convulsion of pop music and wildly different fashions. The generation that had been brought up in the inter-war years would struggle to comprehend the magnitude of social and economic changes that would transform large parts of the western world, including the United Kingdom, forever. Even the "Rhondda Grey" valleys – as Welsh poet and songsmith Max Boyce would later describe them – were to become caught up in the 'ventilation' of people's lifestyles and standards that was at once refreshing to the young and concerning to their parents.

It was in these exciting and progressive times that the Leekes business was continuing to expand with the transfer to Station Yard complete by early 1967. In that same year Llewellyn and Myra's youngest son Stuart became the latest part-time recruit to the business – as soon as he had passed his driving test:

*"I was still at school but my father said, "Well now you've passed your test you can drive the lorry"! Twice one of the wheels came off. On the first occasion, the wheel ran into the police station at Llwynypia and one of the policemen helped me to put it back on. On the second the wheel came off in a street at Trealaw and people who were sitting outside their houses just scattered as it came towards them!"*

*[Stuart Leeke]*

A year later, on 8th August 1968, Gerald Leeke married Sue Edwards at Park End Church in Cardiff. The latest Leeke marriage followed family tradition with Sue and Gerald marrying on a Thursday to coincide with the store's weekly half-day closing – and Gerald even worked in the morning before setting off for the church!

Shortly after their marriage Sue and Gerald purchased the Mill at Hensol which would become their family home, seeing the arrival of their four children, all of whom would later join the family business.

Emma, the first of Gerald and Sue's four children, was born in May 1969 following a midnight dash to Cardiff's St David's Hospital. Her brother Stephen was born in December 1970, followed by Joanna in March 1973 and Christopher in March 1980.

The late Sixties were a busy and significant time for the Leekes business: the plan was to build a new showroom together with a builders yard on the land at Station Yard. This would allow the transfer of both the Brynamlog Yard and the Dunraven Street store plus further expansion to accommodate a similar style of self-service retailing to building and DIY, which had become prevalent in the grocery trade.

By this time they had also moved away from offering discounts to the trade only. Other than quantity discount the selling price was the same for everyone, which led initially to friction with the builders who wanted both credit facilities and discounts. However, due to competitive pricing and the range of products on offer, the opposition gradually faded away.

A start was made by converting the former railway office building into a small shop with the main building being adapted for storage purposes using Dexion racking with a mezzanine floor constructed on top. To keep costs to a minimum, timber for the mezzanine was cut from sleepers found on site using "Big Bertha", a large, 50-year-old circular saw. Ken Thomas, a sub-contractor who lived at Hensol, near Gerald's new home, and who would eventually stay with the business for over 30 years, remembers the activity well:

> "We cut up tons of old railway sleepers which were used as decking for the new warehouse. These were placed on top of the concrete piers. Llew insisted on economy of space everywhere. Everything had to be done properly but, if he could save money on any aspect of the building, he would do so. I didn't always agree with him and I remember that he was always sacking me in those early days. But it wouldn't be very long before we were back together again."
>
> [Ken Thomas]

Cost control was also the prime consideration when developing the new store, right from the planning stage, as Gerald remembers:

> "I approached a Porth architect who insisted on a fee of 5% of the building and land costs, so I asked a friend of Sue's father who worked in Cardiff City Council's architects department to draw up the necessary plans. In view of the need to increase the product range we decided to build the largest possible building we could fit onto the

68

*site on two floors and, to save costs, built it ourselves using*
*sub-contracted labour."*

[Gerald Leeke]

The foundations were dug out by hand, and Gerald, Ken Thomas and Alan Cook remember to this day how hard that preparatory work was. Llewellyn inevitably kept a watchful eye on progress, ensuring a liberal usage of "plumbs", or large stones, in the foundations to save on the amount of concrete needed!

The new building was primarily constructed by sub-contractors, amongst whom a popular group known as the "Valley Boys" provided both character and energy. Gerald's bulldozing drive to get things done was already becoming legendary:

> *"Ivor Parker, the sawyer, was a real character. He always*
> *got frustrated with Gerald's sense of urgency and*
> *nicknamed him 'rip and tear'."*
>
> [Stuart Leeke]

Llewellyn was involved in every way, even supervising the floor screeding and the eventual internal plastering of the new building. Peter Robbins, the plastering sub-contractor, remembers Llew's "careful" approach:

> *"We were using what must have been some reasonable*
> *quality wood battens on window frames prior to*
> *plastering. Llew said that that was no good and we should*
> *use some old battens that were found in the yard. We had*
> *to remove the nails from these before using them and I*
> *remember Llew pointing out that the nails themselves*
> *could be put to good use if we straightened them out!"*
>
> [Peter Robbins]

By the end of the Sixties work had progressed on the new building with some urgency, and the cottages opposite the building had been demolished and cleared to create a car park. During that demolition both Ken and Gerald were involved in a serious accident which forced Ken to be away from work for some considerable time. That drama and other inevitable building delays meant the new premises opened gradually.

At first Station Yard remained a family affair with Llewellyn, his father-in-law David Jones – who travelled down daily from Treherbert – and Alan Cook looking after the yard while Myra, Diane, Gerald and his wife Sue managed the store. It was pretty soon evident that the business could no longer rely solely on family support, especially as the Dunraven Street shop stayed open until 1974:

> *"I remember we had 20 tons of bagged cement delivered at 8am every morning, which Alan and I used to unload by hand. I doubt if either of us has ever been fitter. We would also regularly have a delivery of 10,000 face bricks which again we would unload by hand. God knows what it did to our fingers."*
>
> *[Gerald Leeke]*

Gerald knew the family needed more hands on deck – and quickly. Amongst those who were the early employees of the new-style Leekes business at Station Yard were Emlyn Davies, Tyrone Harris, Ken McGovern, Ivor Parker, Ken Thomas and Robert Williams:

> *"I remember my interview when I started here in 1974. It was with Gerald. It was pretty brief. He simply said, 'do you want a job?' I said 'yes!' then he said, 'ok, start tomorrow!' There wasn't much formality about it."*
>
> *[Tyrone Harris]*

The business's firm family roots remained strong throughout the years ahead; Gerald's wife Sue – besides bringing up their four children – and his sister Diane, with two children, played an important part throughout the expansion of the company being involved in customer service, training, supervising new members of staff and buying for various departments as the business evolved.

Emma, Gerald and Sue's eldest daughter and now commercial director of Leekes, says her mother worked *"incredibly hard"* as the family was growing up.

> *"Our mum ended up working for the business for most of her married life, up to six days a week, from operating the till in Tonypandy to being the decorating and home furnishings buyer for a good ten years – while bringing up the four of us."*
>
> [Emma Leeke]

And the firm retained its family feel – never more evident than at Christmastime, as the first new employees recall:

> *"Every Christmas Mrs Leeke would come around and give each one of us £5 to have a drink and she would always say 'whatever you do, don't tell Mr Leeke'. Then, probably the following day, Mr Leeke would come around and do exactly the same thing. He would give us a fiver and tell us 'whatever you do, don't tell Mrs Leeke'!"*
>
> [Tyrone Harris and Robert Williams]

A recent photo of (left to right) Tyrone Harris, Elaine Baynham and Robert Williams, some of Leekes' longest-serving employees

71

*"I remember every Christmas Eve we would all go to the pub from the Station Yard. Llewellyn would stay in the yard trying to sell the remainder of his turkey tins."*

[Robert Williams]

*"Alan and Gerald were always available to give a hand with any heavy work if we were busy. However, at Christmas time we always had drinks with them up at the Monkey Club. This was always a dangerous time and inevitably I got home late.*

*"One Christmas after Llewellyn had had some health problems we had a function, and I think it was at the Green Down Inn, in the Vale of Glamorgan. Llewellyn was not supposed to eat cakes but was hiding behind one of the pillars. He said to me, 'if you get me a couple of those cakes, I'll buy a round of drinks for the whole table'. I pretty soon got him a plateful of cakes which he seemed to enjoy!"*

[Tyrone Harris]

*"I remember every Christmas my father would give everyone at Tonypandy a chicken. Either my father or Alan would collect these from Megan Price at Ynysallyn Farm near Llantrisant. This was a present everyone liked – it created a great, friendly atmosphere."*

[Diane Leeke]

The official opening of the new premises was given considerable coverage in the *Rhondda Leader* on Friday 24th August 1974:

*"There are showrooms on two floors: the downstairs floor which has recently been converted to self-service and the upper floor with kitchen fittings, bathrooms and fireplaces on display . . . Obviously in a self-service store a far greater quantity and range of goods can be displayed than with counter service. Leekes has a staff of 15 employed in both*

72

*showrooms and the building yard where the firm stocks large quantities of materials such as sand and cement. They are open every day of the week, and if you don't happen to want to take your purchases home with you, their transport will deliver to your door.*

*"With the fast pace of modern living, the handyman and builder of today wants to spend as little time as possible shopping for materials. At Station Yard you will find just about everything you could need from a paintbrush to a new bathroom suite – all under one roof."*

*[Rhondda Leader]*

The retail concept was, in some ways, not entirely different to the old days at Court Street with a multiplicity of items sold under one roof. But now the previously so-called 'cash sections' were essentially self-service and the total range of products and services were much more extensive and much more upmarket. Fitted kitchens and bathrooms were offered through a range of household names, some of which are still around today: Gower and Hygena kitchens and Ideal Standard bathrooms could all be fitted in customers' homes, set off by a range of Cristal wall tiles or Marley vinyl floor tiles. With Leekes it was possible to *"enrich your home with a Courtland fireplace"* or have a Parkray heating system fitted to service a newly-installed shower unit. The exclusive Hygena Kitchen Studio at the store was seen as something very special for Tonypandy at the time.

The Rhondda now had a store which offered every conceivable product and service that the electrician, carpenter, plumber or glazier might require. For the budding DIY-er the new store fed the growing belief that anyone could do a professional craftsman's job with the right tools. The concept was a huge success and pushed the business further away from the limited *"We Are Grate People"* image. But Llewellyn's commitment to his customers stood firm:

73

*"Llewellyn was always keen to satisfy the customer. His motto was always to take any order that came in and to try and deliver it that day if possible. If not we would ensure it was delivered the following day."*

[Tyrone Harris]

The way the business took off is simply astonishing. Increasing customer demand and interest were further fuelled by better product design, better packaging and marketing – and of course better pricing, offered through bulk purchasing. Ceramic tiles were still an important element of the business and as customer demand grew so did the orders – but Llewellyn was still sceptical when Gerald ordered the first 20-ton delivery of the best quality tiles!

The Tonypandy store was one of the very first new-style DIY outlets, to be followed of course by many national success stories of companies who used similar retail concepts, such as B&Q. It was generally acknowledged that the DIY market was going through the kind of process that the grocery market went through in the '60s, and Leekes was at the forefront of these changes. By 1975 the Dunraven Street store had been closed and the success of the new-style store was clear with turnover reaching £½ million.

Of course not everyone was overjoyed by this hard-won success which capitalised on the growing DIY trend. Supplier H R Johnson, for example, at that time the UK's leading tile manufacturer, came in for some industry criticism due to the discounts being offered but, to their credit, continued to back Leekes. Even the Builders Merchants Federation was critical as many of its members were suffering. The customers, of course, were very happy with such a comprehensive DIY service, driven on by special magazine articles and courses to encourage even the most ham-fisted handyman to have a go!

With larger markets clearly emerging outside the confines of the Rhondda, the search now began to find a site for a new, larger store in the Llantrisant area to take the business another major step forward. But more of that later . . .

In 1988 the Rhondda Taxis premises in front of Station Yard were purchased. After a long-running dispute, planning permission to extend was finally granted.

David Jennings, Tonypandy store manager, and Mike Davies, deputy store manager, at the Rhondda Taxis site at the time of the planning dispute

Members of the Leeke family at the Tonypandy store with the Mayor of the Rhondda at the store extension opening

The new extension to Station Yard was officially opened in March 1991 by the Mayor of the Rhondda.

The family and the business remained committed to the community in which Leekes had been first established and frequently supported local worthwhile causes.

Mrs Myra Leeke, store manager David Jennings and a representative of Dulux Paints present a cheque for £1400 raised for Rhondda Special Schools by Leekes' Tonypandy store with support from Dulux

# Chapter 5

# LLANTRISANT –
# THE FIRST SUPERSTORE

The economic decline of the Rhondda continued throughout the Sixties and Seventies; and a number of government reports on the future South Wales economy, along with the extension of the M4 motorway, identified the Llantrisant and Pontyclun area as a favourable location for residential housing and, if necessary, a retail centre. The fact that the Leeke family was living nearby at Groesfaen brought the added benefit of local knowledge to the acquisition of a site for a new store.

A number of alternative locations were investigated including land at Coed Cae Lane in Pontyclun and at Ynysmaerdy, near the Royal Mint and around what would much later become the site of the Royal Glamorgan Hospital. All these options were declined by the planners.

John Collingridge, who was then working for South Wales-based furniture manufacturer Christie Tyler and was a friend of Gerald's, mentioned that his company had been looking at the former Staedtler Royal Sovereign Pencil factory to convert into an upholstery factory but had decided against it. The factory, which had been empty for some time, was to become a good choice for Leekes' next phase of expansion.

The main factory, built in two separate large units, had been occupied by Staedtler since 1946 when the company moved from its former base at Neasden in northwest London. Wales had, at the time, been one of the government's designated development areas and the company had chosen the 17-acre greenfield site. However, when John Charnaud, managing director at the new factory, returned from wartime duties he discovered that things

The Staedtler factory site in the 1950s, later to become the site of Leekes' Llantrisant store. The large unit on the left became the Leekes store at Llantrisant and Pontyclun Van Hire is on the right

A recent aerial photograph of the Llantrisant store, showing both units and the link created between them as well as the furniture showroom to the rear

weren't quite as they had seemed. No government aid was forthcoming as Staedtler had made a sizeable profit from the sale of the London factory, and building permission was initially only given for manufacturing, with no facilities for administration. Despite those teething problems the building was completed by George Wimpey and Sons in 1947 and Staedtler became – and still remains – a notable employer in the area.

John Evans, the present managing director of Staedtler, remembers Charnaud as an engaging local character who would frequently travel to work on horseback, refreshing his horse in the water trough which today would be located opposite the garden centre entrance to the Leekes store.

By the early '70s the demand for manufacturing efficiencies and the installation of new technology prompted Staedtler to move to bigger and better premises and it built a new, state-of-the-art factory on its land at the rear of the old buildings. In 1973 Wingate Investments purchased the original factory which remained empty for a year or two while new lessees or purchasers were sought for the six-and-a-half acre site.

Leekes initially bought one of the units and opened its store in August 1977 while the second section was occupied by the local Evans family as a base for their transport business, Pontyclun Van Hire. Smaller units were occupied by a number of firms who would, in due course, relocate elsewhere.

The purchase was not without a multitude of planning problems. These were the days before out-of-town shopping centres existed, so retail premises were invariably situated in town centres. Local residents were unhappy about the potential parking problems and some of the neighbouring companies also expressed concern about the traffic difficulties which would ensue. This meant that many councillors on the local authority planning committee were not inclined to give planning permission for the new venture. It took many meetings and many hours of persuasion by Gerald and Llewellyn plus the considerable support of local Councillor Tudor John – who was particularly keen to see the derelict factory become a source of employment – to convince the planning authority and unhappy councillors. To purchase, convert and open the store a substantial initial investment was required and Gerald's next battle was, not surprisingly, for financial backing:

> *"For the first phase at Llantrisant I forecasted that we needed an extra loan facility of £350,000. I approached Lloyds, who had been our bankers for over 50 years, but, amazingly, all sorts of obstacles were put up. Then a cricket friend, John Davies (JA), who was a bank manager, arranged a meeting with the regional director of Midland Bank. We met the following Tuesday and the deal was concluded over a handshake after lunch. Eventually, due to the immediate positive cashflow we generated, the facility was never utilised but due to the excellent service we received we have retained the same bankers (now known as HSBC) right up to the present."*
>
> *[Gerald Leeke]*

This start of a new era for Leekes coincided with a period of optimism in the UK. 1977 was just one year after James Callaghan, a Cardiff MP, had taken over as Prime Minister. Callaghan – known as "Sunny Jim" – was always upbeat about everything. The economy was strong and he told the country all was fine. Not even the deaths in that year of icons Bing Crosby and Elvis Presley darkened people's spirits; it was, after all, the year of the Queen's Silver Jubilee and there was a multitude of celebrations and street parties. While punk rock exploded onto the music scene and the Sex Pistols reached number two in the charts, it was a year when most people were still wearing polyester flares and thought they could dance like screen god-of-the-moment John Travolta.

For Gerald the Abba hit from that year *"Take A Chance On Me"* would prove most appropriate; local customers were clearly prepared to do so and were actually telephoning weeks before the store opened to ask when they could start to shop. However, there were a few weeks of hard work to be done first.

One of the first to be recruited at the earliest stages of the opening of the new store was Ralph Theaker. Ralph had previously worked at the Pontyclun Joinery Company, which later became known locally as Capeners. He remembers well the incredible cleaning operation to clear the residual graphite dust from the old pencil factory, with local painting contractor Ted Prosser spraying red oxide paint as work continued, to make the old factory more presentable for customers. The usual hands-on approach was adopted by the family and its growing number of employees to turn the factory into a store:

> *"When I joined, shortly after the first part of the old Royal Sovereign Pencil Factory had been bought by Gerald, I remember the huge amounts of graphite dust which was everywhere. Everyone had to help in clearing up. I remember seeing Sue Leeke with a turban and a black face . . . [from the dust] . . . helping to clear up."*
>
> *[Ralph Theaker]*

With all hands on deck, the new store eventually opened for business within a few days of contracts being signed and the unit being taken over, with plenty of alterations still going on as people shopped. The astounding public interest in the store surprised everybody:

> *"When the store first opened the customer parking situation was a nightmare. The tankers visiting our premises next door at Purolite couldn't get in at weekends. We were forever trying to find owners of cars. Eventually we simply had to put bollards down and employ someone wearing a white coat to prevent people parking on the access to our premises. The interest was incredible."*
>
> *[Purolite Plant Manager Dai Davies]*

*"It was amazing the number of people that came to the store in the first few weeks. We simply had to work around customers. You have to remember there were very few suppliers in this area and serious builders would have to go to Cardiff or Tonypandy. The growth was so quick that we were always moving partitions and walls. I think it would have been easier if we had put some of the walls on castors!"*

*[sub-contractor Cyril Vaughan]*

This was a totally new experience for the South Wales shopper, and Llewellyn was justifiably very proud while remaining ever the shrewd businessman, according to family friend Les May:

*"The Llantrisant store was very futuristic when it opened. It was the first DIY store on that scale in South Wales. The displays were tremendous for the time. You could look at five or six manufacturers at the same time. It was great for the customers . . . Shortly after the Llantrisant store opened Llewellyn took my wife and I around on a guided tour. He was so proud of the new venture. He was always a stickler for cleanliness and when he spotted a small pile of rubbish on the floor he went to collect one of the new brushes that were on sale and cleared this up. He then proceeded to clean the brush itself and return this to its rack – that was typical of Llewellyn."*

*[Les May]*

Once open, 20 new jobs were very quickly created within the store. The initial team included Mike Bessant, Wayne Davies, Kitty Evans, Phillip and Roger Gooch, Steven Jenkins, Peter Mundell and Sue Viggers. They would later be joined by Jim Williams who was the manager responsible for kitchen sales, and Andrew Morrison in the DIY section.

*"When I joined everything was a bit of a shambles. One of the first big jobs we had to do was to put down terrazzo tiles and this had to be done whilst we were serving customers at the same time."*

[Peter Mundell]

Kitty Evans was Gerald's first secretary and she remembers well the speedy expansion of everything – as well as her boss's infectious energy and can-do approach:

*"When I left commercial school I tried to join Leekes at Tonypandy but there were no vacancies at that time. I eventually joined in 1977 as Gerald's secretary. I remember explaining that I couldn't operate an Olivetti computer. Gerald simply said 'have a go'. I did and he thought it was okay and I subsequently stayed 15 years. The early years at Llantrisant were chaotic. There were simply too many things going on at the same time. I can remember sitting in the office at the same time that its wall was being knocked down!"*

[Kitty Evans]

The small administration and accounts department was headed up by Phillip Jordan who had Diane Evans, Mary James, Hilary Lewis and Linda Davies (later Foster) in his team. Gerald's keen accountant's eye was as focused on cashflow as every other aspect of the business as its expansion continued:

*"When I started in the accounts department it was my first real job after school. It was really great fun. I remember on one occasion I arranged to pay a big account before it was due. I think it was Hotpoint. I remember Gerald asking me if I had enough money in my piggybank to pay him back. I suppose that's why I'm still working here!"*

[Linda Foster]

New sections were soon established. John Demmer would eventually join to manage the electrical section and James Edwards joined from Great Universal Stores to set up a new furniture department. This was a departure which was new to the core family business and Gerald recognised the importance of getting the right people in position:

> *"I believe Llewellyn thought I was a bit of an oddbod. He tended to stand at arm's length from the furnishing department. This was a new world to him."*
>
> *[James Edwards]*

> *"James's background in furniture retailing was invaluable to us. I think James could sell sand to the Arabs. He was initially involved in selling kitchens until the furniture department grew."*
>
> *[Gerald Leeke]*

By the time of the official opening in September 1977 the Llantrisant store was now labelled a "DIY Superstore" and the company could realistically boast that this was now the biggest and the best self-service DIY store in South Wales. Initially there were 10,000 square feet of storage space in the converted factory and some 20,000 square feet of selling space with shelves full of tools, paint, tiles, timber, ironmongery and everything else a handyman might need. Outside there were more buildings devoted to the company's other speciality – builders supplies, such as cement, timber and plaster.

> *"Eventually we had an official opening for the Llantrisant store. Max Boyce was the main guest at that opening and I remember it was at a time when the Wales rugby team were at their peak. We all wore badges with 'I was there with Max'. It was a great day."*
>
> *[James Edwards]*

With Gerald's concentration on the Llantrisant store further help was now required in running the Tonypandy store. His younger brother Stuart was persuaded to leave accountants Panell Fitzpatrick where he had trained since leaving school in 1969, and he joined the company in 1977. Together he and brother-in-law Alan Cook would run Tonypandy until 1983 when he would relocate to the Llantrisant store.

Llewellyn Leeke now had two successful operations to keep an eye on and he usually split his day between Tonypandy in the mornings and Llantrisant in the afternoons. The scale of the new operation sometimes bewildered him but his attention-to-detail in areas of familiarity remained legendary:

> *"In the early days at Llantrisant we were still selling enormous amounts of tiles from boxes. There were no displays available at the beginning. Tiles were simply sold on measurement. Llewellyn was always cagey about this and if the area measured came to three yards, he would advise the customer to call it four because 'you always break a couple'. Similarly if, say, three gallons of adhesive were needed for a particular job, Llewellyn would always advise that they take four. He was some salesman!"*
>
> *[Alan Cook]*

While there was no problem encouraging customers through the doors, expansion efforts could not escape the inevitable acts of God and simple accidents:

> *"We seemed to have every disaster you could possibly imagine during the first few years. We seemed to survive the 'great freeze', then we had the 'great flood' when all the drains couldn't take the water and old graphite waste was discharged back into the store. All the carpets were ruined. Then on another occasion I remember the roof collapsing; it was a lively place to work."*
>
> *[James Edwards]*

*"On one occasion a young employee, I believe it was Glen Kidner, drilled through a water pipe near the double glazing area. To stop the water flowing, he climbed up a ladder and kept his finger over the hole. Unfortunately for him Gerald walked by and asked him what he was doing. Despite protestations he insisted on Glen climbing down the ladder. Naturally, as soon as he removed his hand, water spurted out everywhere. Inevitably Gerald climbed up the ladder instead of him and tried to hold the flow. It was hilarious!"*

*[Cyril Vaughan]*

By the end of the Seventies the main departments at Llantrisant were DIY, the builders yard, kitchens and bathrooms. Gower, Schreiber and Hygena supplied kitchens and also a limited amount of freestanding bedroom furniture; in fact, the store had already become the largest kitchen retailer in Wales, but the extended range of kitchen displays meant there was a constant pressure on space.

The store had grown quickly and expansion was still moving at a rate of knots, with Gerald remaining typically hands-on as he drove the business forward, resolutely ever-present – whatever it took, according to staff:

Ralph Theaker shows Henry Cooper how to drive a fork lift truck at the official opening of the new DIY and building departments in the original unit

*"Llantrisant just seemed to grow every month. There was no planning involved – we just used the space that was available. It was simply 'just try a few products and we'll see how we get on'. It just grew from that."*

[Roger Ragg]

*"The pace of things was tremendous but it was great fun. There was a really great spirit in those early days. I think Gerald would go home in the evening and dream about some change. Then we would be expected to get on and do it the following day! The style was very much 'just build it' and we'll draw the plan afterwards!"*

[Dennis Wattley]

*"When I joined Leekes at Llantrisant I was only 17 and I remember everything had to be handled manually. I was moving a huge pile of plasterboard and dropped it onto Gerald's foot. I thought I would be in serious trouble but he took it well, even though his foot was badly bruised and swollen. I remember that they were pushing him around in a shopping trolley for the rest of the day!"*

[Phillip Gooch]

Everyone else was expected to be as adaptable as the boss; having employees prepared to turn their hand to whatever needed to be done was crucial in such a fast-growing business – and created a great team spirit:

*"When I first joined Llantrisant you needed to be very flexible. It was completely different to Cardiff City Council where I had previously worked. One minute I'd be interviewing a buyer near the bathroom section and the next I would be helping a customer; after dealing with the customer I'd then return to the buyer."*

[Roger Ragg]

*"Everything seemed to expand so quickly. Because we were all such a new team we formed a fairly close community. We still have longstanding friendships that last even until today."*
*[Linda Foster]*

*"The friendship and the characters and family spirit are the things I remember most from the early days. There were frustrations but you tend to forget those as you get older."*
*[Dennis Wattley]*

This team spirit was boosted by regular social events, with the close-knit atmosphere of a family business remaining as the business and employee numbers grew:

*"There was a tremendous social spirit in those early days. I remember we used to have treasure hunts which would usually be organised by Alan Cook. We would always end up at Gerald's house for a barbecue, a few barrels of beer and a disco. It would be unusual if somebody wasn't thrown into the swimming pool by the end of the evening. They were great times."*
*[Ralph Theaker]*

*"After Mr Llewellyn Leeke had bought his Rolls Royce he arranged to collect me from home to go to a company Christmas party at Driscoll's in Porth. I remember I was wearing a pink dress for the occasion but didn't realise until Mr Leeke arrived that his new Rolls Royce was also pink. Goodness knows what we looked like!"*
*[Kitty Evans]*

But true-to-form, even at Christmas, Llewellyn Leeke's ever-commercial head still didn't take a complete break, this time with a wider range of last-minute purchases on offer than Dunraven Street's turkey tins:

> *"On Christmas Eve we would all arrange to go off to the*
> *pub when the store was closed. Mr Leeke Senior would*
> *always stay behind, explaining that most men usually buy*
> *their wives presents late on Christmas Eve. There would*
> *always be some panic purchases and he would stay behind*
> *just in case."*
>
> *[Kitty Evans]*

The store had proved a great success right from the start and in 1980 company turnover reached £4 million – and still the rapid expansion continued. By 1981 the first dedicated furniture department had been established in the newly-built first-floor extension at the rear of the store. Much of the extended range on display was made by local upholstery manufacturer Christie Tyler. Other, national manufacturers continued to be somewhat sceptical of displaying high quality, high value products within what they saw as essentially a DIY store. James Edwards well remembers travelling with Gerald to London to be 'interviewed' by representatives of one of the UK's leading manufacturers, G-Plan, to establish whether Leekes would be allowed to sell their furniture. At the end of the meeting the G-Plan representatives concluded *"We'll let you know whether you can sell our products"*: James remembers well Gerald's riposte which was simply *"And then we'll let you know whether we want to sell them!"*.

> *"There was undoubtedly an image issue with some suppliers*
> *who were unsure whether their products and a DIY and*
> *'builders merchant' were compatible. Unfortunately it was*
> *sometimes difficult for the 'Rhondda Ironmonger', as I was*
> *frequently called, to become a stockist for some of the*
> *branded manufacturers. I went to a lot of meetings before*
> *success initially with Christie Tyler and G-Plan. Gradually, as*
> *more of them came on board, the others quickly followed."*
>
> *[Gerald Leeke]*

To help them make their decision perhaps some suppliers would have been interested to see for themselves the ever-increasing flow of customers. While it was, of course, the lifeblood of the growing business, growing demand caused some practical headaches – dealt with, as ever, in the most practical of ways:

> *"The parking outside, of course, was impossible and we used to issue warnings to customers over the tannoy system at Llantrisant telling them whenever traffic wardens were around."*
>
> *[Roy Colenutt]*

> *"From time to time we would have problems with shoplifters. We used to have a special code call where the girl on the central desk would send a tannoy message asking for 'Mr Sidney Leeke' to come to the till. Everyone on the staff in the store then knew that some shoplifting would be going on. Everyone available would then rush to catch them. We frequently had to chase them through the car park and on some occasions follow them by car until the police arrived."*
>
> *[Ralph Theaker]*

Despite the reticence of certain suppliers the furniture department's growth was extraordinary. James was soon supported by Julia Billington and David Jones as part of his sales team. His staff would eventually extend to include Fred Lewis and Gordon Mainwaring and, a little later, Ken Jones, formerly a sergeant in Coastal Command and a professional boxer. Sales of bedroom furniture in particular were hugely successful and Gareth Davies, who had previously worked for his father's company Beddy Buys, joined as the first professional bedroom furniture salesman and buyer. Huge demand soon saw double glazing and sportswear added to the store's departments:

> *"One of the very first double glazing contracts we had was for Sir Geraint Evans who lived in Aberaeron. This was for*

*13 windows and a door in the early 1980s. I don't know how we got the contract but it was seen as a prestigious installation."*

*[Cyril Vaughan]*

As its reputation grew many potential employees saw Leekes as an opportunity for career development. John Sullivan, previously a charismatic sales manager for Schreiber, became the first sales manager at Llantrisant in the early Eighties, by which time the store had moved on considerably from those very early days in 1977 in the way it presented itself.

In 1981 the second unit was purchased and an extension built to join it to the first within a year and a new main entrance built between them. The new unit was used for furniture and kitchen displays – although it had first been required for a rather more unusual purpose:

*"The business expanded so quickly that it wasn't long before we took over the second unit at the old pencil factory. However, before we actually occupied this we were asked by the local Jehovah Witnesses if they could use the premises for a convention of over 500 to hear a preacher from the US. Gerald agreed to this but we were obliged to make some token attendance to offer our support. It was a really incredible experience."*

*[James Edwards]*

Gerald Leeke takes up the story of Llantrisant's swift growth:

*"In the early 1980s, even though our furniture sales were continuing to grow, I felt, from visits to furniture supplier showrooms, furniture exhibitions and other retailers, that our furniture displays would have to improve in order to take advantage of the new space available in the showroom and achieve our full sales potential.*

*"Luckily, through competing against each other on the cricket field, I had become friendly with Nigel Phillips who was the sales and marketing director of Christie Tyler, the largest upholstery manufacturer in Europe and one of our key suppliers in the early days. He was delighted to help and, during a visit to London for a furniture show, introduced me in the Café Royal to Terry Jones, a freelance designer who had successfully completed a few projects for his company.*

*"Terry designed a superb American-style gallery for upholstery which doubled sales within months and would later become the model for furniture retailers all over the UK.*

*"Terry was soon to become directly employed by the company, and his design flair and ability to adapt to the wide range of projects and challenges thrown at him since have proved invaluable and made him one of the key components in its success."*

[Gerald Leeke]

Boxer Howard Winstone cuts the ribbon to officially open the newly extended Llantrisant store joined by local officials, Leeke family members, SuperTed and the Dulux dog

Chairman of Christie Tyler, George Williams, opens the new Leekes Furniture Gallery with Gerald, Terry Jones and Nigel Phillips of Christie Tyler

Mr and Mrs Leeke Senior were both still active in the business, with Llewellyn continuing to work mornings in Tonypandy and afternoons in Llantrisant. But in December 1982 the family and the employees were to mourn Llewellyn's sudden death at St Winifred's Hospital, Cardiff following a heart attack after an operation. With a remarkable work ethic and an aptitude for business which was second-to-none, he had been a true entrepreneur throughout his life and, having run the business for over 50 years, he had been immensely proud of the rapid expansion since Gerald joined the firm in 1966.

Llewellyn's funeral was conducted by the Rev. A W Rees at St David's Church in Groesfaen on 21st December 1982, followed by cremation at Glyntaf Crematorium in Pontypridd. The following year, on 16th October, a window in the church was dedicated in memory of Llewellyn in recognition of all the support he had given to St David's and especially to Myra while she was church warden between 1965 and 1980.

*"When Father joined the business full-time in 1925 one of his first tasks had been to open a builders yard in the same way that, 40 years later, one of Gerald's first tasks was to develop Station Yard. For 57 years Father was at the forefront of the business, becoming Chairman and Managing Director when the company was formed in 1956.*

*"When he died in 1982 he was still fully involved in the family discussions taking place to decide where the next store should be located in West Wales."*

[David Leeke]

In the spirit which Llewellyn had embodied, Leekes' expansion continued just as rapidly. By the mid-1980s the number of employees topped 100; by the late Eighties company turnover had increased dramatically to over £30 million from less than £100,000 in the early Seventies. The breakdown of that turnover showed that, while a significant percentage of sales volume was due to the DIY sector and the traditional building trade, the growth in kitchens, bathrooms and particularly furniture was astonishing. The Llantrisant store would now be carrying around 50,000 different products amounting to £500,000 in value at any time – and smart staff uniforms were a far cry from the simple builders merchant days:

*"I remember Mrs Leeke Senior coming into the bathroom section at Llantrisant and seeing me in a floral patterned shirt. She said, "You look like a Hawaiian wine waiter". I knew from that moment we were bound to get staff uniforms. The first uniforms we had were in 1988 or 1989. For the men it was a green blazer, a white shirt and a green-and-white striped tie. Very smart at the time, although I'm not sure about now."*

[Paul Collier]

The number of displays available and interior design service offered were sufficient to satisfy the most discerning of customers. The Llantrisant store could now lay absolute claim to have moved on from being a DIY superstore to being a true "out-of-town department store", as it was soon to be labelled in extensive marketing campaigns.

Leekes had truly blazed a trail and many other well-known, national companies quickly followed. The exclusivity of much of the retail sector, with retailing primarily taking place in town centre specialist shops, was broken down, and Leekes was at the forefront of the now much-talked-about retail boom. As ever, the solution to the next problem – this time the fast encroaching competition from the supermarket giants – was resolutely practical and speedy:

*"Once Tesco had opened in Talbot Green the competition in certain DIY products became very intense. They were using Dulux paint as a loss-leading promotion and selling it much cheaper than us. This was the start of the big grocery supermarkets expanding their product range. We talked to ICI, the manufacturers, but they couldn't help. When Tesco dropped the price even further we found we could buy cheaper from them than ICI. Gerald arranged to send a lorry to Tesco to purchase as much as we could get. We practically cleaned them out of stock and Tesco became alarmed. From then on they seemed to charge realistic prices."*

*[Roger Ragg]*

*"We decided to attend more trade shows looking for new products. Being a keen sportsman I felt that a sports department would attract extra customers and be a good use of some available space. We looked at sports clothing at several of the London shows. In those days just to get onto a Nike or Adidas stand you needed to be an account holder; all the stands had a staffed entrance and the representatives*

*emphasised their own importance by booking appointments! We solved that by 'breaking into' the back of the stand. It seemed to work. How things have changed!"*

[Gerald Leeke]

The growth of the Llantrisant store continued with the opening of a new golf department in May 1991 by Ian Woosnam, barely a month after he became the world number one and scooped his first major tournament – the US Masters at Augusta National Course. He spent over an hour at the store giving demonstrations of how to hit a golf ball, telling anecdotes and signing autographs, much to the delight of the 400-strong crowd.

Ian Woosnam getting to grips with that famous swing

Left to right: John Sullivan, David Leeke, Stuart Leeke, Ian Woosnam, Mrs Myra Leeke and Mostyn Thomas

As ever, the fine line between the Leekes business and the family was blurred when there was something to celebrate – and Mrs Myra Leeke's 80th birthday celebrations on 14th June 1993 were no exception. She can be seen here enjoying a party with friends, family and Llantrisant store staff at Gerald and Sue's family home at Hensol.

Leekes becomes one of the largest Welsh firms to be awarded Investors in People, presented by John Phillips, chairman of Mid Glamorgan Training and Enterprise Council

Long service at the Llantrisant store is not confined to employees outside the family: Gerald's sister Diane Cook has worked there throughout the 30 years since its opening. She had started her career with the company in 1961, when she helped David run the business for eight months while their father was ill.

Gerald and Mrs Myra Leeke with George Best in 1997 celebrating the Llantrisant store's 20th anniversary

Llantrisant employees with 20 years' service pictured in 2004 (left to right), back row: Mark Goody, Vaughan Davies, Gareth Davies, Graham Euston, Ann Honey, Tony Rees; front row: Nichola Goody, Chris Thomas, Phil Gooch, Rhonda Worgan

She then continued to work in the Dunraven Street shop until it closed in 1974, while at the same time bringing up two young children, later transferring to Station Yard where she ran the decorating department.

When the Llantrisant store opened in 1977, Diane took on the responsibilities of supervising the tills, training cashiers, organising banking and dealing with the customer queries. Later she helped set up various departments including lighting, the cook shop, mirrors and pictures and the store's first restaurant.

Now a board director of the Group, Diane still enjoys working after, incredibly, 46 years. She is currently its longest-serving employee and aims to complete at least 50 years' service.

# Chapter 6

# GO WEST, YOUNG MAN

In the early Eighties the economy was buoyant. This new decade brought the 'Thatcher Years' when that strange business and social animal the 'yuppie' was first sighted. "Cool" young office types made a fashion statement by wearing their jackets with the sleeves rolled up, while teenagers' T-shirts declared "Frankie says . . ." or urged "Choose Life".

It was the Rubik's Cube era, a time when you could choose Betamax or VHS tapes for your video recorder. It was the birth of home computing when the Spectrum computer, whether for business or games, was every smart home's must-have accessory.

At this point the enormous success of the Llantrisant store indicated to Gerald that the time was right to look for another site. Leekes' market research had shown that customers frequently travelled up to 40 minutes from within Wales to visit the Llantrisant store; so the search was now on for a location in West Wales at double that drive time, so that the two stores would not compete against each other.

A number of alternatives were looked at, usually by Gerald, John Sullivan and Ken Thomas. Options around Swansea included the developing Swansea Enterprise Park. However, the Leekes team decided that too much competition would soon be on its doorstep in Swansea.

The next location considered in detail was Carmarthenshire. Geographically, the town of Carmarthen, at the junction of the A40 and A48, seemed an ideal site with good access for customers from Llandeilo, Lampeter, Cardigan, Swansea and also Haverfordwest in Pembrokeshire. Tentative negotiations began in connection with a possible site but these eventually broke down.

In the meantime it became apparent that the population of

Cross Hands and its hinterland was higher than that of the Carmarthen area; it was also on the route to Swansea for the whole population of South West Wales – as far as Fishguard and Cardigan – which they routinely visited for their major shopping. Cross Hands was also famously noted as a traffic bottleneck for people travelling from the east towards West Wales.

The site was finally purchased in 1983. It had previously belonged to the National Coal Board (NCB) and had been strongly promoted by Llanelli Council, although there were some doubts regarding its suitability due to local underground workings. Eventually a survey was undertaken and the purchase agreed, although the original planned location of the store had to be altered within the site. Work commenced immediately on the considerable clearing operation to remove millions of cubic metres of shale and coal dust before building could begin.

By now the coal industry was in steep decline and the NCB wanted to close 20 pits, which would have left 20,000 men jobless. Arthur Scargill, president of the National Union of Mineworkers (NUM), called for industrial action and on 12th March 1984 a strike began which was to last for nearly a year. Ken Thomas, who supervised the building work at the Cross Hands site, remembers that 20 or 30 local miners were employed for labouring work and they were enormously grateful for some income to supplement their meagre strike pay.

Eventually the miners acknowledged defeat, returning to work on 5th March 1985 after what had become one of the most bitter disputes of the 20th century, and the South Wales coal industry continued to decline, with 12 pits closing within a year of the strike coming to an end. This further reduction in the mining industry bore remarkable similarities to the early days of this story in the Rhondda Valleys.

Despite that difficult background the atmosphere during the development phase of the Cross Hands store was one of excitement and optimism: there had been nothing like this in the area before, as one of the first employees recalls:

*"To call it "Leekes of Cross Hands" was a clever marketing move. The local emphasis certainly put the village on the map. Prior to Leekes arriving there was simply nothing here. We even used to get mail on some occasions addressed simply to 'Leekes of West Wales'. It was amazing."*

*[Mike Brotherwood]*

Local company TR Jones Limited was appointed as the initial builder with steel fabrication carried out by Condor Buildings. The store was constructed in a series of modules with the buildings put together in three stages and, for some of the later phases, another company, Hereford-based Miffling Construction, was used.

The construction work was not without its problems. Apart from the challenge of building on old mine workings Ken Thomas recalls three large truckloads of bricks being enthusiastically and beautifully laid to accommodate the conservatory area. When the fourth load arrived in a totally different colour all the initial work had to be demolished and a restart agreed.

While the buildings were under construction the publicity programme started. Lyndon Thomas of Cardiff-based LWT Marketing began his long association with Leekes at this stage, heralding the company's more strategic approach to marketing. In the weeks prior to opening a newspaper drop was carried out, delivering to households throughout the whole of West Wales. Printers Wiltshire's of Bristol received their largest ever order to produce 250,000 copies in both Welsh and English to be delivered all over Swansea, Carmarthenshire, Pembrokeshire and as far away as Aberystwyth – and a new TV commercial was conceived:

*"The first time we used the "Out-of-Town Department Store" strapline was after two days filming a commercial with Windsor Davies. Windsor was extremely popular at the time as a result of the success of "It Ain't Half Hot Mum". At the*

*end of the commercial the strapline was inserted and has been used ever since. We had come a long way from the first attempts at marketing with the "We Are Grate People"!"*

*[Lyndon Thomas]*

Paul Beddoe, one of LWT's marketing managers, was heavily involved in the opening and, with expenditure on advertising and marketing increasing rapidly, would join the company a few years later to head up a new, in-house department.

Recruitment was typically speedy with Gerald's mind unswervingly focussed on opening as soon as possible as one of the first recruits remembers:

*"When they were planning the Cross Hands store I was working for a competitor across the road. One day a yellow Mercedes drove into the yard and out stepped two gentlemen. I didn't know at the time but these were Gerald Leeke and John Sullivan, the first manager at Cross Hands. They told me they were opening a store across the road. There was nothing there at that moment. A few days later they called back and asked me if I was interested in a job. It was all pretty casual."*

*[Colin Garnett]*

As ever, it seems, with a Leekes superstore to get ready, inevitable mishaps occurred in the rush to open the doors, as staff member Alan Price witnessed:

*"I remember some weeks before we opened deliveries were coming in thick and fast and rubbish was piling up all over the place. TRJ, our contractors, were told to start a fire out the back and burn some of the cardboard boxes. We had to do this quickly because of an imminent inspection from the fire officer. There were all hands on deck to get rid of these boxes; the only trouble was not all of them were empty.*

*Ten video players were among the boxes and they weren't noticed until one of the contractors frantically tried to get them out of the flames."*

[Alan Price]

Then, just a few weeks before the opening ceremonies, an open valve in the water supply to the building created a flood during the night; when Gerald and Ken Thomas arrived the following morning they were greeted by a torrent of water pouring out of the building. The internal damage was heartbreaking but, with typical Leekes resilience, everyone simply got stuck into a major clearing up and drying operation. Fortunately the opening day did not have to be postponed, but this was certainly a problem the Cross Hands workers could have well done without – as deputy store manager Paul Collier recalls:

*"The scene was incredible but the camaraderie amongst everyone to recover the situation was fantastic. Everyone was involved. Gerald was very impressed with the way everyone got stuck in."*

[Paul Collier]

The store was opened on Friday 5th October 1984 by Ian Kelsall, then the head of the Wales Confederation of British Industry (CBI), together with the mayor of Llanelli and other local dignitaries.

The following day Gerald, Max Boyce and Super-Ted arrived by helicopter in the car park for the "Grand Opening" of West Wales' biggest "Home Improvement Centre". There had been nothing like it in the area before, but the public reaction amazed even hardened retailers like new store manager John Sullivan; the crowds and traffic brought Cross Hands and the surrounding area to a standstill. More than 6000 people had been waiting for the special guests and around 15,000 passed through the doors on this first day. Even the well-travelled Max Boyce had seen nothing like it.

Long traffic jams at the opening of the Cross Hands store in 1984

They even managed to almost – but fortunately not quite – stop the wedding of local couple Phil and Janet Evans at Gorslas Church just a mile away. The store was quick to make amends for the other big day they inadvertently nearly spoiled, as one of the Cross Hands store's first employees recalls:

> *"I remember on the opening day the crowds in the area were incredible. The young couple were delayed an hour getting to the church and, by the time the bride arrived, I understand the bridegroom was pretty nervous. When we found out about this we presented the couple with a tumble dryer. John Sullivan made a great fuss and apologised for the inconvenience. We had a great relationship with them thereafter."*
>
> *[Colleen Thomas]*

The furniture, kitchens, bathrooms, tiles, decorating, electrics and DIY sections were inundated, and the garden centre and builders yard also welcomed streams of inquisitive customers. The restaurant ran out of food and the staff were exhausted by the end

The presentation of a tumble dryer to newlyweds Phil and Janet Evans with, centre, store manager John Sullivan and staff members Colleen Thomas and Clive Bowen

of the day. Employee Anne Hinkin remembers the experience of preparing for and working over the opening two days:

> *"When I joined on the Monday there was nothing available in the catering section: just four walls and a cooker. They then told me that we were going to open the following Saturday. I nearly panicked. We had a separate opening on the Friday for local councillors, the mayor and other dignitaries. About ten minutes before they arrived we were still polishing everything. Anyhow we got through that okay but the following Saturday it was just unbelievable. The crowds came from everywhere and you couldn't move."*
>
> *[Anne Hinkin]*

People had come from all over the west, from as far away as Lampeter, Milford Haven, Haverfordwest and Cardigan. The excitement continued throughout the first full week of trading and many from the Llantrisant store staff team travelled to Cross Hands to help. By the end of that week, few people in West Wales were unaware that Leekes' second superstore had arrived.

Regular special events with guest celebrities were held at the store and continued to boost its popularity – although these didn't always go without a hitch according to Paul Collier:

> *"I remember on one occasion for some event at Cross Hands we had booked Vinnie Jones. He was one of the stars of the Welsh football team at the time. He was playing somewhere near London on Saturday and was due to fly in by helicopter on the following Sunday from Luton. The crowds in the car park were massive but unfortunately Luton Airport became fogbound. As store manager at Cross Hands I didn't know whether to face everyone or run! Fortunately for me Paul Beddoe [Leekes marketing director] . . . pulled a few rugby contact strings and managed to get a few stars like Jonathan Davies along to save the day. This placated everyone, thank goodness."*
>
> *[Paul Collier]*

Local sporting celebrities were also among the shoppers and, on more than one occasion, they used their particular talents to help out:

> *"I remember when a shoplifter was chased by Irwyn Gilasbey across the store. "Glaz", I believe, was playing number eight for Llandeilo at the time. He managed to tap the guy's ankle and restrain him. At the time Ray Gravell, one of Wales' favourite rugby stars, was shopping in the store. He said, "Do you know, that's the best ankle tap I've seen all season"!"*
>
> *[Paul Collier]*

> *"We used to have so many competitions against Llantrisant after we opened. We were not very good at squash or badminton in Cross Hands. I remember that Barry Brookes*

*arranged for a couple of boys from the local club to help us. Gerald couldn't understand how we then beat Llantrisant. One of those boys of course was the Welsh international squash champion Adrian Davies. That's how he and Gerald met."*

[Anne Hinkin]

Over 20 years after its opening Leekes Cross Hands' staff's overriding impression of their local customers is one of lasting loyalty:

*"We still have a number of customers who just come here almost everyday for a walk and a look around the store and possibly a spot of lunch. We always seem to have a strong relationship with the locality."*

[Anne Hinkin]

*"I know some of our customers who came here when they were children, probably aged six or seven, with their parents. They are now coming back themselves with their own children."*

[Colin Garnett]

Max Boyce joins Gerald, Mrs Myra Leeke, Cross Hands store manager Paul Collier, and the Mayor of Llanelli to celebrate the store's 10th anniversary in 1994

In 1997 Jonathan Davies – accompanied by elder daughter Grace – officially opened the new Sports and Golf Department at Cross Hands with Mrs Myra Leeke and Gerald

Leekes' tradition of supporting their local communities continued with the opening of the latest store. Right, store manager Stuart Mainwaring helps local schoolchildren with their garden project with tools and plants donated by the Cross Hands store in 2001

Cross Hands employees with 20 years' service pictured in 2004. Back row, standing, left to right: Peter Mundell, Steve Morgan, Colin Garnett, Alwyn John. Middle row, seated, left to right: Gareth Rowlands, Paul Heyel, Anne Hinkin. Front row, seated, left to right: Sheila Williams, Colleen Thomas, Aileen Pyle

# Chapter 7

# CROSSING THE BRIDGE – THE OPENING OF MELKSHAM

About seven years after the Cross Hands store opened Gerald began looking at developing another new store which, using the same formula as Cross Hands in order not to compete with the existing stores, would need to be 80 minutes' or so travelling distance away. Various options were considered but it soon became obvious that, in order not to compete and have sufficient population within easy travelling distance, it needed to be over the Severn Bridge. Various options were considered throughout the county of Wiltshire, and eventually some 12 acres of land became available at Semington near Melksham. The land was bought on the understanding that the local authority would give planning permission for a large retail store. However, due to a change of ruling party following local elections, it eventually became apparent that the new administration was not going to grant planning permission and the land was eventually sold off.

An alternative parcel of land, adjacent to the busy A350 road through Melksham, had belonged to the Spencer Iron Casting Company. The company had closed a few years earlier and Tull Investments, a local firm, was dealing with the disposal of the land and buildings on its behalf. The site was felt to be the perfect location for Leekes' fourth store, being within 45 minutes' drivetime of 2.5 million people living in Bristol, Swindon, Chippenham, Bath and Salisbury and around 80 minutes from the Llantrisant store. After a three-year search the purchase was agreed in 1991, and Ken Thomas and his team set about demolishing some of the existing casting buildings. In true Leekes style some of the materials from the old warehouses at Melksham were eventually transferred to the group's head offices and distribution centre at Mwyndy near Llantrisant where they would be reused in the construction of warehouses.

The general concept for the Melksham store, which incorporated a glass-domed atrium and piazza, was put together by Gerald, Terry Jones and Ken Thomas, and well-known South Wales building firm Evan G. Jones was awarded the building contract. When built the £5 million store would be over 160,000 square feet on an eight-acre site with parking for 850 cars.

Ken remembers the many hassles overcome during this project. Apart from the building itself Leekes was required to construct a roundabout at the entrance to the store for traffic control. A zebra crossing had to be moved and, possibly most complex of all, various underground cables had to be relocated, including a large fibre optic cable used by the Ministry of Defence. All this added tens of thousands of pounds to the cost of the Melksham project.

The site itself was extremely wet and required additional drainage. On the first few days of building site-traffic became bogged down in the wet soil. The winter of 1991 was extremely cold – arguably not the best conditions for constructing a prestigious retail store on a complex site. In addition there were some problems with the second floor whose 'suspended' construction was a completely new concept in buildings of this sort. Other unfortunate difficulties included four of the original contractors going into liquidation during the course of the project.

The site had been used informally for all sorts of local events while vacant. Once building started Ken Thomas remembers being called by the police one evening because thousands of young people were holding a rave in the old crane buildings that had been used by the casting company. Ken went across to the site and, apart from being amazed by the number of drink cans littered around, could see no fundamental damage being done and realised that, in any case, his ability to stop the event would be fairly limited. The project proceeded regardless of all these issues, on schedule and to increasing local interest: after all, as Ken Thomas remembers one of the local planning officers explaining, the building's total square footage would be greater than Melksham's entire existing retail square footage. Inevitably some local traders watched events with caution.

For some contractors the new store was a prestigious project: Tetbury Steel, which undertook the steel fabrication work, was part of a worldwide construction group and would show their international visitors around the site to demonstrate their capabilities. The location resembled a tourist attraction rather than a building site, as Ken Thomas remembers, when 20 or 30 Japanese potential customers for Tetbury arrived and photographed everything that moved! When they returned after a boozy lunch a long queue soon formed outside the site's single Portaloo.

The Melksham store nearing completion, above right

Recruitment was the by-now familiar story: it was done quickly, informally and the team spirit was immediate, with all hands on deck to get the store open as soon as possible:

> *"I don't know how they did the recruitment for everyone prior to the opening. It was all done at a bit of a rush and very informally. I remember that they offered me a job, then later I was interviewed, then finally they asked me to fill in an application form. I think it should have been the other way around."*
>
> [Steve Cossey]

> *"The first management team was John Sullivan and Peter Mundell. They were a good partnership but very different characters. John Sullivan always seemed to pop up if anything went wrong. He certainly knew all the staff and at the end of each day he would stand at the door thanking everyone.*

> *"Peter was the assistant store manager and was always available. He was fanatical about cleaning up and always wanted the store to look good."*
>
> [Steve Cossey and Sally Oatley]

The store opened on 12th August 1992, just about a year after Gerald, Ken and the rest of the team had begun examining the site. There was one final panic immediately before opening when a fire started from some rubbish stacked against the back wall of the building, which brought back memories of a similar fire before the Cross Hands opening some eight years previously and required an emergency clean-up before guests could be received.

Officials from the local authority planning department together with the fire officer visited the building in the early hours of the morning for their final inspections. Although the planning officers had some concerns the fire officer declared his satisfaction and approval and, with a huge sigh of relief, the planned arrangements for the opening could proceed.

Well-known TV presenter Leslie Crowther had been invited to open the store. His appearance, together with the general excitement of one of the largest retail projects in the county of Wiltshire, ensured that the police would have a very busy time trying to control the crowds and traffic.

The opening of the Melksham store with Leslie Crowther and store manager John Sullivan

Leslie Crowther leads a throng of customers into the store on opening day

The store's layout, which comprised 20 mock shopfronts, gave the appearance of stand-alone concessions but all departments were owned and run by Leekes. They included *The Rhondda Trading Company*, selling occasional furniture; *Banana Village*, selling ethnic accessories; and *The Oriental Import Company*, selling lightings, ceramics and furniture from the Far East. As part of its promotion 200,000 36-page brochures had been produced and distributed throughout three counties and around 30,000 visitors came to the opening with at least 2000 in-store at any one time. Just like at Cross Hands a decade earlier, this locality had seen nothing like it before, as employee Joyce Walker recalls:

> *"The restaurant simply couldn't cope on the opening day when Leslie Crowther came. It was all very exciting for us. This was the biggest thing that had happened in Melksham for donkeys' years."*
>
> *[Joyce Walker]*

Gerald had stayed on site to change into a suit to welcome the many guests, but Ken had returned to smarten up at the hotel at Corsham where they had been staying during the later days of the construction. By the time he came back to the store the police were stopping the huge volume of traffic, which by now had blocked all the surrounding roads, and told Ken that he could not proceed. Fortunately, after parking his car elsewhere, the man who had been heavily involved in the project right from the outset was able to rejoin the celebrations.

The new store proved an immediate success despite opening when the country was in the grip of another deep recession. The final stage of the Melksham store development came with the opening of the builders and tradesmen centre celebrated in November 1992 with a freefall display by the Red Devils parachute team. Within a few months the store was making regular deliveries through Hampshire and Dorset and down to

Devon and Cornwall – then finally to the London area as well; customers from as far afield as Reading and Bournemouth were returning time and again.

> *"You must remember that this concept was completely new for the Melksham area. People could come to the store, walk around and have something to eat if they wanted to. There were hours of interest for people here."*
>
> *[Joyce Walker]*

The understandable initial scepticism of local traders was quickly dispelled, with the shoppers' enthusiasm easily matched by one local businessman:

> *"When Melksham opened a lot of the local traders benefited enormously from increased trade. I remember one café owner put an advertisement in the local newspaper thanking the Leeke family for the hugely positive effect everything had had on his business. Before the opening day 140 lorries arrived delivering goods on one day alone. That meant a lot of sales of cups of coffee and sandwiches for the café owner!"*
>
> *[Lyndon Thomas]*

Towards the end of the year the first-floor bedroom department was extended to a massive 16,000 square feet with 21 bedroom settings, and the finishing touches were put to the new soft furnishings department. At the end of its first year of trading, shoppers' appreciation of the Leekes retail concept was confirmed when a £14 million turnover was reported.

And so, 112 years after the birth of James Henry Leeke, his grandson had ensured his first, strong commercial foothold on English soil, bringing a new shopping experience to Wiltshire and its surrounding counties.

To celebrate Leekes' first anniversary at Melksham, a week of cookery demonstrations, competitions and personal appearances

– including Dino the Dinosaur and rugby star Jeremy Guscott – was planned. According to Group marketing director Paul Beddoe the store wanted to celebrate by creating a party atmosphere at Leekes with something for everyone. As at Cross Hands, special events drew more crowds and spread the word even more widely for the new store – even if there were a few hiccups along the way, as staff member Lyn Sharman testifies:

> *"We still get many personalities coming into the store. In the early days it was exciting to see TV personalities such as Roger Cook and Derek Fowlds. There were sports personalities like Jeremy Guscott and loads of people from soap operas. On the fifth birthday we even had George Best here. Sometimes not everything went as planned. On the first birthday I remember that the Red Devils parachutists dropped into the car park but one of them landed in a tree and broke his leg!"*
>
> *[Lyn Sharman]*

George Best and girlfriend Alex join Melksham's fifth birthday celebrations in 1997 with marketing manager Stephanie Metson and sales director Stephen Leeke

Paul Collier recalls the George Best visit where the queues for his autograph were increasing and he reminded him he was due to leave:

> *"His reply was that he was staying until everyone had been seen as that was what his visit was all about."*
>
> *[Paul Collier]*

Since opening in 1992 Melksham has gone from strength to strength, and continues to be a destination for shoppers from all over the South West of England.

The Melksham store's loyal employees who joined Leekes at the start in 1992, pictured in 2004. Left to right, back row: Simon Bridgford-Whittick, John Miller, Nick Hilbert, Karon Hay, Paul Trenchard; front row, left to right: Mike Smith, Clive Clutterbuck, Lyn Sharman, John Beacham

*Chapter 8*

# A NEW HEAD OFFICE
# AND CENTRAL WAREHOUSE

In the early 1990s, with the business continuing to develop and grow, the resultant increase in stock and customer deliveries arriving at the individual warehouses at each store was putting them under severe pressure.

In 1993 an opportunity came up to purchase a site on Mwyndy Business Park, just three miles from the Llantrisant store. It was being vacated by the builders Evan Jones who had links with the Leekes business through being involved in the construction of the Melksham store.

At first this facility, which comprised offices and warehousing on a ten-acre site, was used to hold the Llantrisant store's customer orders prior to delivery. In addition Leekes had developed a successful double-glazing business in partnership with Rhondda-based firm Sky Aero. Together the companies had formed a joint manufacturing venture using a small warehouse in Treorchy and, as that unit became too small for the needs of the fast-growing business, production was moved down to the Mwyndy warehouse.

With continued growth in sales across the stores, the business began to employ more people and the support functions such as personnel, marketing and design, IT, finance and accounts also started to grow. These teams, along with the buying team, had been based on the first floor above the store at Llantrisant. As numbers grew it was clear that those offices were becoming too small.

At the same time, while the use of the Mwyndy warehouse for Llantrisant's customer deliveries had been successful, the warehouses at Cross Hands and Melksham were still struggling to cope with their increasing deliveries. So the decision was taken to centralise the warehousing and deliveries for all the stores at

Mwyndy and also to move all the buying teams and support staff there from their cramped offices at the Llantrisant store. And in late 1994 the move was made.

The centralised warehousing and delivery operation was initially run by Alan Cook, who retired in 1998. When he had first joined the company in 1964 he recalls that his job description was officially 'odd job man' because he was expected to deal with any task that arose. One such task was delivering orders in the pick-up truck, and he soon obtained a Class 2 licence, which qualified him to drive the 10-ton lorry, frequently into Cardiff at 6am to collect a load of sand. In the late 1960s, soon after the move to Station Yard, he became yard foreman before taking on the role of stores manager in the mid-1980s. When the warehousing and delivery operation was centralised at Mwyndy Alan was appointed distribution director and when he retired in 1998 he had given the company 34 years' service.

Following Alan's retirement the business employed a well-known local character Dai Davies (or "Dai Dogs"). Dai knew the company well having worked for the chemical business Purolite, whose premises had been next to the store in Llantrisant, for over 20 years. With Purolite moving production from the Llantrisant site Dai was looking forward to his retirement before Gerald sought him out one night at his local pub, The Ivor, in Pontyclun, to offer him the challenge of running the warehousing and logistics for Leekes. Dai accepted and started virtually immediately. In his initial few months he unearthed lots of "forgotten" stock which had been moved from the individual stores as part of the centralisation process.

> *"I particularly remember Dai calling me down to the warehouse following a check of fireplace stock when he claimed to have discovered 'more marble here than at Glyntaf cemetery'!"*
>
> *[Gerald Leeke]*

Llew and Myra's youngest son, Stuart, had started his career with the company working alongside his brother-in-law, Alan

Cook, to run the Tonypandy store when Llantrisant opened in 1977 and Gerald transferred there. In 1979 he became the first of the Leeke sons free to marry on a day other than Thursday. The growth of the business was such that staff could now hold the fort while family members attended special occasions without having to close. So, on Friday 7th September 1979, Stuart married Celia McCormack at Llanishen Parish Church. Two years later their son Matthew was born, followed by daughters Rachel in 1984 and Rebecca in 1989. By 1983 Stuart had also transferred to the Llantrisant store and was appointed a director and company secretary.

Besides running the payroll, with the rapid increase in numbers of staff, Stuart took responsibility for setting up and running the new human resources department and still today works closely alongside the human resources director. His duties involve looking after the staff in all respects, from the monthly payroll and employee benefits to the social side of the company. In addition, Stuart organises all the company insurances and transport, and is known for his early starts – 7am, his first task being to join Gerald in opening all company mail.

Centralisation was also an opportunity to strengthen the management team and over the next few years a number of key appointments were made, both from within and outside the family, which would introduce new ideas and fresh enthusiasm.

In September 1994 elder son Stephen became the first of Gerald and Sue Leeke's four children to join the family business, as a management trainee after graduating from Sheffield University with a degree in Business and Spanish. Although all four siblings work for the Group today, Stephen says there had never been any firm plans for any of his generation to join Leekes.

*"We always knew opportunities would be there for us should we want to make our careers in the business, but there was never any active encouragement let alone pressure to take them up.*

> *"I'd been at boarding school* [Tockington and Sherborne] *from the age of six, didn't want to go to London and was excited by the chance to live in my local area. I also knew that I would be able to get stuck into work where I could make a difference – which I did. I was fortunate and I was immediately hooked – this being the hands-on business that it is I had real experience and responsibility straight away, far more so than I would have had as a graduate trainee within some faceless multinational."*
>
> *[Stephen Leeke]*

Stephen's first project was the unenviable task of achieving ISO9000 accreditation for the double-glazing manufacturing business, which he delivered within 18 months. He later joined the Board as sales director for Leekes although his future would lie not in retail but in the leisure side of the business that Gerald was soon to begin developing, and he would go on to become the managing director of the Vale Resort in 1998.

It was just before the launch of the Vale Resort in October 1999 that Mike Fowler, the Leekes Group finance director, joined the business after qualifying as an accountant at Deloittes in Cardiff. In typical Leekes fashion, he had to hit the ground running.

> *"I was thrown in at the deep end in that I had to set up all the accounting systems and controls for the new hotel business in a matter of weeks!"*
>
> *[Mike Fowler]*

Mike's next task was to modernise the departmental system of accounting on the retail side of the business so that the profitability of each could be accurately measured.

> *"There were a few surprises with some departments more profitable than expected while some buyers soon realised theirs weren't quite turning the profit they thought."*
>
> *[Mike Fowler]*

Profits increased rapidly as financial controls and procedures improved and accurate, up-to-date information improved the buying process.

Soon after joining Mike continued the Leekes tradition of working hard and playing hard by joining in the bi-weekly games of squash where Gerald has often expressed his pleasure that Mike is *"thankfully better at running the accounts department than he is at keeping score on the squash court"*.

Joining the board of a family business could be daunting for some, but not Mike:

> *"It is refreshing to work in an entrepreneurial environment where decisions are made quickly without all the usual red tape. It's also a bonus that everyone works well together and has a bit of fun as well while making tough decisions too."*
>
> *[Mike Fowler]*

Joanna Littlejohn was the next family member to join the business, at the dawn of the new millennium in January 2000. Gerald and Sue's younger daughter, she joined as a merchandiser after working in London for five years, beginning her career in retail by working in men's accessories for Top Man, and gaining experience across a number of roles before becoming a senior merchandiser for Top Shop coats.

Jo's first role at Leekes was to work with the buying team, instructing them on the use of the information gathered by the EPOS system, where items are scanned at the checkout, to influence buying decisions. She then began buying for the fitness department, later expanding her role to also oversee buying for the DIY and building departments.

In July 2001 Stephen and Joanna were joined in the business by their sister Emma, the oldest of Gerald's four children. Emma had joined Marks & Spencer as a graduate trainee following her degree in Business and spent a total of ten years with the retail giant, working in some of its largest stores around London including a period of time managing her own stores. As her intention was always to return to work for the family business, she decided to expand her experience with M & S by transferring to their head office in Baker Street where she was a buyer for a wide variety of products including ladies lingerie and men's coats and trousers. With a small son, James, and a daughter, Olivia, on the way, Emma and her husband, Mark, a solicitor originally from Birmingham, had decided that the time was right to move back to Wales where she would join the family business.

When Emma joined Leekes in 2001 as commercial director, it was clear that there were fantastic opportunities to apply many of the store operations and buying skills she had learnt. While it was important to retain many of the unique attributes of the family business, it was clear that there were many areas where a more professional approach would reap rewards. There followed a full review of the business operation and key areas for strengthening were identified, resulting in a review of the structure and the recruitment of some key, experienced personnel. One major focus was the sourcing of products: under Gerald's personal direction Leekes had been one of the first UK independent retailers to actively investigate the new areas of furniture production around the world, with him leading visits to the Far East as early as the 1980s. Emma further developed this and the buying team began to explore global sources for a much wider variety of products, including ceramic tiles from Spain, Middle Eastern bathroom ranges and teak furniture from Indonesia. This enabled the business to retain its competitiveness across all its departments against the growing onslaught from national retailers.

Just a year after Emma joined the Leekes Board, Peter Martin was appointed as human resources director after relocating from London with his Welsh wife Maria and their five young children. He was a clear choice for the role, although one of his interviewers did comment that the business 'may struggle to keep up with him'!

Peter's responsibilities within the business soon grew and now include management of store operations where he enjoys keeping the teams on their toes with his early morning starts and detailed floor walks. He is a great fan of using bottles of wine as incentives for store managers to hit various targets and has been known to challenge a store manager to hit a £200,000 sales growth target for the grand prize of a £4.99 bottle of red!

Peter's great sense of humour is seen by his Board member colleagues as a definite asset when under pressure – although some victims of his elaborate wind-ups may not agree. Just after Gerald received his OBE from Prince Charles in 2006, Peter had a quiet word with Cross Hands store manager Peter Mundell to say that the Prince may be 'stopping off' during a visit to Carmarthenshire to see the Leekes business for himself. Peter swore his namesake to secrecy 'for security reasons' but charged him with making sure the store looked pristine in time for the royal visit. He then proceeded to let the rest of the store staff in on the ruse so they could watch in amusement as Peter Mundell raced around the store demanding that they sweep the paths, install fresh plants at the entrance, tidy up the displays and even put flowers in the men's toilets. Peter made sure he was safely 60 miles away when he called the store manager – who was surrounded by his staff team – to confess!

The last of Sue and Gerald's children, Christopher, joined Leekes in January 2003, starting in the logistics department where he implemented a system to deal with faulty or unwanted goods and completed a project to improve in-store stock management systems. Like his siblings Chris had in fact been working for Leekes in various roles for some time, first in the summer of 1994 as a labourer helping delivery drivers in the builders yard at Llantrisant. After that he tried his hand at a variety of roles to earn some money during school or university holidays, including labouring on the Vale Hotel construction site, working at the Mwyndy warehouse and as a silver service waiter in the hotel. Since 2003 his already varied experience of the family business has seen him run the Tonypandy store and oversee firstly a complete IT systems review and then its implementation.

Most recently, in December 2005, Matthew Leeke, Stuart and Celia's son, joined the company. He had graduated from Bath University with a degree in Economics and Politics and had worked in the House of Commons as a researcher during his placement year. Since joining Leekes Matthew has been a senior member of the team developing e-commerce, the company's latest venture which, using Sainsbury's experiences as an example, could well increase turnover as much as the opening of a new store.

Over time the central head office and warehouse have proved to be major advantages for the business. As manufacturing increasingly moves overseas, the business has been able to use its buying power to purchase stock in container quantities from all over the world in order to maintain its competitive pricing and cater for those customers who want immediate delivery of items from stock.

Leekes' Mwyndy-based staff celebrating more than 20 years' service in 2005. Left to right: Richard Berry, Pam James, Paul Collier, Linda Powell, John Thomas, Linda Foster and Roger Ragg

With an increasingly complex organisation to control and with a number of senior experienced managers now employed in key roles, Gerald decided to formalise decision-making with the formation of an executive board who would meet away from the distraction of the busy stores and head office on a monthly basis. The meetings have proved a great success and the ability to have fresh views and ideas from experienced individuals not directly involved in a particular issue or problem has proved to be very helpful to all concerned.

The Leekes Group Executive Board pictured at head office: from left, Terry Jones, Emma Leeke, Peter Martin, Mike Fowler, Gerald Leeke, Stuart Leeke, Paul Beddoe and Stephen Leeke

*Chapter 9*

# A COMPLETELY DIFFERENT RACQUET

While it enjoyed huge growth through the Eighties and into the early Nineties, the J H Leeke Group invested significantly in supporting the local community through a variety of good causes but especially with sports sponsorship. This sponsorship was initially through local schools and local rugby and football sides near to the individual stores but soon progressed to an involvement with leading rugby clubs such as Cardiff, Bridgend, Llanelli and Bath as well as with Wales's premier football club, Cardiff City FC.

Their first major national sponsorship, however, was the creation of the Leekes Welsh Wizards professional squash team in 1988. The American Express-sponsored National League had started in 1984 with ten elite teams – all English – and included the top 20 squash players in the world. Players such as Pakistani legends Jahangir and Jansher Khan, Australians Rodney Martin, Chris Ditmar and Chris Robertson, ex-world champion Ross Norman and top UK stars Del Harris and Mark MacLean were soon to be regular visitors to the Wizards' home at Cardiff Squash Club.

Prestigious venues throughout the UK formed the league with well-known, very established clubs including Edgbaston Priory, Lambs of London, Cannons, Chapel Allerton and Manchester Northern (the Wimbledon of the North).

Adrian Davies, then Welsh number one professional player who was playing for Manchester Northern, and Robert Edwards, the Cardiff businessman who was also the Wales national team manager, joined forces to try and create the first non-English national league team. Between them they created a sponsorship package and presented it to Gerald and Paul Beddoe, the Group marketing manager, and The Leekes Welsh Wizards were conceived.

Their proposal was to enter a team into Division Two of the League and, once the negotiations had been successfully concluded with Leekes, Robert and Adrian contacted the custodians of the sport, The Squash Racquets Association of England (SRA), based in London's Old Bond Street.

The SRA had initially declined entry from teams outside of England but pressure and influence from John Petersen, the Vice President of American Express, Europe, overturned this objection. American Express was the very important sponsor of not only the British National League but all the regional county and local squash leagues. More significantly John was from Cardiff, the son of famous boxer Jack Petersen, the British and Empire Heavyweight Champion in the 1930s, and he emphasised to the SRA that, from a marketing viewpoint, his company would benefit from greater exposure with a Welsh team featuring in the leagues.

What was to happen next could be termed at best sneaky and, at worst, one of the dirtiest tricks imaginable! Upon filing the entry, Robert and Adrian were stunned to be informed by the SRA that all the Division Two teams had reapplied (for the first time in the five years of the competition) and there was now no space for a new team in the lower division. However, space remained in the Premier League but a new entry had to be filed within 48 hours. The SRA of course knew that, while a second division side would consist of three or four semi-professional players with one world-class player, a Premier League team would have to comprise five full-time professional players on the world circuit just to survive – and these players commanded much higher appearance money.

So Robert and Adrian's only option was to endeavour to sign up four other world-class players within 48 hours in order to form a team for entry to the Premier League, and to even begin to attempt this required a four-fold budget increase. Kitty Evans, Gerald's PA at the time, arranged a meeting for Robert and Adrian to break the news.

As Adrian had already informed Manchester Northern he was leaving and had handed his sponsored car back to them, there was a lot at stake for him both professionally and personally. Sixteen years on, he recalls that meeting with both amusement and amazement:

> *"I think I felt more nervous going into that meeting than I did two years later going into the final of the European Championships. Gerald welcomed us into his office and asked us why the urgency for this meeting. Typically, there was no small talk. He got straight to the point. Robert went into his usual articulate flow and explained that it was basically a case of 'the English trying to stitch us up'. Inevitably that struck a competitive chord with Gerald. His pointed retort after Robert's long explanation was simply 'we'll 'ave 'em'!"*
>
> *[Adrian Davies]*

The meeting then got down to business with Robert and Adrian explaining, not without some embarrassment, that the £25,000 sponsorship that Gerald had agreed to only 24 hours previously would need to be increased to £100,000 if they were to proceed.

The silence in the meeting seemed to go on forever with Gerald rocking back and fore on his office chair contemplating whether this presented a liability or just a tougher challenge. Adrian remembers well what happened next:

> *"Just to break the awful silence I jumped forward and offered my hand saying 'I'll be in the top ten in the world within six months which will give the company even greater publicity!' Gerald then simply said 'yes' and got up and walked out of the room. Robert and I sat there for about 20 minutes wondering where the hell he had gone. When we enquired with Kitty she explained, 'it's Friday night, he's gone off to play squash'!"*
>
> *[Adrian Davies]*

That was it – the Wizards were born although no business detail had ever been discussed. As far as Gerald was concerned it was a done deal. For the next eight years the agreements followed the same pattern; no letters were exchanged and no contracts. The most exciting innovation in UK professional squash continued on a handshake.

Desperate calls were made to players who might not have signed contracts for the forthcoming season. Gawain Briars – former England captain and world number four, was living in Nottingham and at first thought it was a hoax, apparently a regular occurrence on the squash circuit. Only four days earlier he had been accepted onto a law course in Cardiff. In total disbelief he informed Robert that Ricki Hill, the son of a south Australian pig farmer and now a captain of Virgin 747 jumbo jets, was also available.

So, rather hurriedly, along with Cerryg Jones (former Wales captain and top thirty world player) and Darren Mabbs, Avon county semi-professional, the team was complete.

In October 1988 the Wizards' campaign began: they lost their first match 5-0 away in Colchester and their second match was a 4-1 loss at home. They ended their first season last in the league.

To progress changes had to be made and four of the five original players were replaced. Only captain and original Wizard Adrian Davies was retained, and four new players, an Australian, Chris Robertson, a Scotsman, Mark Maclean, a Canadian, Jamie Hickox and an Englishman, Rob Owen – all world top 30-ranked – were recruited.

By the end of the second season the Wizards had swapped bottom for top and *The Times* in December 1989 gave them a glowing review. In 1990 the Leekes Welsh Wizards were voted the BBC/Western Mail Wales Sports Team of the Year, beating the higher-profile rugby, football and ice hockey teams who had all had very successful seasons – and all this achieved in just three seasons.

When Adrian was on his way to the German Open in 1989 Gerald asked about the set-up of a professional squash

Leekes Welsh Wizards 1989/1990 British Team Champions (L to R): Chris Robertson, Mark MacLean, Adrian Davies, Robert Edwards, Rob Owen and Jamie Hickox

tournament. Once Adrian had explained how it worked Gerald asked why he couldn't have one of those in Wales. Adrian replied tongue-in-cheek, *"You can. All you need is a glass court, 64 world-class players, at least $80,000 in prize money, hotel accommodation for a week for all players, 16 referees, event insurance and so on."*

His jaw dropped when Gerald simply responded *"We'll have one of those then!"* and promptly dispatched Robert Edwards and Paul Beddoe on a fact-finding mission to the Dutch Open at The Hague. Paul remembers:

> *"One minute I was working on the Leekes winter sale advertising, the next minute I am in Holland trying to work out how we would run a world-ranking squash tournament – absolutely surreal!"*
>
> *[Paul Beddoe]*

So, in February 1990, the Leekes Welsh Classic Squash Tournament was born. In true Leekes style, this tournament was launched as an important first – $102,000, the biggest prize money in the history of squash.

*"The entire Leekes senior management was drafted in and every part of the staging and running of the event was dealt with in-house – a true example of learning as you went along. We also wanted to open up the sport to a wider audience and ensure that other sponsors had opportunities to entertain their guests. We therefore decided to launch the first event with a black tie gala dinner at Cardiff's magnificent City Hall. With over 400 guests and entertainment very appropriately provided by the Rhondda's Treorchy Male Voice Choir and the Cory Band the evening was an outstanding success. The squash fraternity, used to low-profile events, albeit all over the world, just couldn't believe their eyes!"*

*[Paul Beddoe]*

Not only did the event – held at the Welsh Institute for Sport in Cardiff – set new standards for squash tournaments throughout the world, it also carried with it by far the best ever worldwide television coverage of the sport, thanks largely to a local producer named Aled Roberts who worked for the BBC. Local interest was maintained as Adrian steadily progressed through the early rounds to set up a mouth-watering quarter-final with one of the greatest players ever to hold a squash racquet – Jahangir Khan. After losing in a five-set thriller an exhausted Adrian bumped into his personal sponsor expecting to be praised for his performance only to be forthrightly told by Gerald *"you blew it!"*.

*"The 1990 Leekes Classic was the first time we had worked with national television and before the event*

*started we arranged for the Leekes logo to be printed on the floor of the squash courts. The BBC lawyers simply wouldn't accept this. They told us that unless the painted logos were moved within one hour they would pull the plug on televising the event. Hearing the news, Gerald simply disappeared from the sports hall laughing, leaving me with angry lawyers and BBC executives. Within one hour the logos were painted out and we had a team drying the paint with hairdryers!*

*"Martine Le Moighan, the Guernsey-based ladies world champion, complained that she was picking up green paint on her shoes. By this stage I was completely exasperated and simply told her to "play or the BBC pulls out, and so will our sponsorship". This she certainly did and went on to win by three games to one!"*

*[Paul Beddoe]*

Gerald Leeke with world champion Jansher Khan and ladies world number 2 Sarah Fitzgerald at the Lord Mayor's official reception for the Leekes Welsh Squash Classic at Cardiff City Hall.

Adrian Davies speaking at the banquet at Cardiff City Hall to celebrate the first Leekes Welsh Squash Classic in 1990

Let's not forget that Leekes was still a family business and the professional players and TV companies were not the only ones with concerns. When the event was launched the *Western Mail* mentioned the record $102,000 prize money and Stuart Leeke, the company secretary, received a telephone call at 7.30am from his mother – then well into her 70s – extremely concerned to read that the company was giving $102,000 *"to some squash players – what on earth is going on?"*. To avoid any future issues Stuart decided the best course of action would be to reassure his mother – who had of course been such an important part of the company for so many years – that it was a misprint and should read $10,200: if only she had known that the total staging budget was £280,000!

In 1991 the tournament became the first major sports competition to be held in the brand new Cardiff International Arena, and similar events followed over the next three years. The tournament was often voted 'Event of the Year' by the world's leading players for the way they were looked after by Leekes and the people of Cardiff in the true tradition of Welsh hospitality.

Celebrating Leekes' £¼ million sponsorship of the British Open Squash Championship and the staging of the tournament outside England for the first time (1995): (left to right) Paul Beddoe, marketing manager for Leekes, Derek Gadsby, chairman of the Welsh Squash Federation, English SRA committee member Stuart Courtney, Wales Number One and PSA vice chairman Adrian Davies, Gerald Leeke and Andrew Evans, Welsh Squash Federation director of coaching and development

In 1994 Leekes made an audacious bid to poach the ultimate squash championship, the Wimbledon of the squash world – The British Open – from the custodians of the event, the SRA, and stage the event outside England for the first time in its 78-year history. It was rumoured that the then Chairman of the SRA, Sir Michael Edwards, was heard to comment the event would only go to Wales *"over his dead body"*. Adrian Davies and Paul Beddoe made the trip to London, presented a convincing argument and the British Open was on the way to Cardiff – despite Sir Michael's protest.

In 1995, 1996 and 1997 the Leekes British Open brought some 500 competitors from over 50 countries to Wales. The event again set new standards, using two glass courts for the first time ever, charity black-tie gala dinners were held, bigger crowds were present and record takings were achieved for both ticket and merchandising. All this which, at the beginning, must have been seen simply as the piracy of a traditional English event, became what is now regarded as the most successful series of international squash tournaments ever staged.

The 1996 Leekes British Open Squash Championship, held at Cardiff International Arena

In addition IPM, the company Gerald had set up to manage the TV coverage of the first tournament in 1990, had gone from strength to strength. It had soon won the TV rights to cover all the top squash events, including a three-year deal with Sky Sports and other worldwide broadcasters. Leekes personnel were soon enjoying trips to exotic places including Hong Kong, Qatar, New York, Amsterdam, South Africa, Egypt and Pakistan and the events were now seen by a worldwide audience of over 300 million. The players benefited enormously from the extra exposure and the sport had come a long way since Gerald was persuaded to sponsor a squash team!

## Chapter 10

# ... AND NOW FOR SOMETHING COMPLETELY DIFFERENT: THE VALE RESORT

In June 1994 the sports sections of the *South Wales Echo* and the *Western Mail* were dominated by plans for a £12 million sports and leisure complex covering 200 acres at Hensol, near Llantrisant. They reported that the existing nine-hole golf course, driving range and surrounding parkland were set to be transformed into a prestigious sporting complex, complete with a further 18-hole golf course, a lakeside hotel, leisure club and centres of excellence for squash and tennis:

> *"South Wales businessmen, headed by Gerald Leeke, managing director of the Leekes out-of-town department store, are joining sporting personalities to launch the venture, which is covered by an earlier planning permission".*
>
> [source: Leekes press announcement]

The shareholders in this new consortium included former England and Glamorgan cricket all-rounder Peter Walker, Robert Hodge and John Saunders of Cardiff-based Hodge & Company Corporate Finance, and British Swimming Association coach and ex-Olympic swimmer David Haller. Founder shareholders Peter Johnson, who had formerly been the professional at Cardiff Golf Club, and Ginny Golding, who was working with the Welsh Golfing Association, would continue as director of golf and director of administration respectively.

That was the first public announcement of plans to ensure that the Vale of Glamorgan Golf and Country Club – as it was originally known – would become one of the leading sporting complexes in the UK.

The earlier planning permission had been secured by local landowner Howard Joyce who, having retired from his extensive garage and other business interests in South Wales, had astutely invested in the purchase of various parcels of land throughout the Vale of Glamorgan.

One of those parcels included almost 200 acres of farmland surrounding the 17th century Hensol Castle which, supplemented by the construction of a number of ward buildings, was being used as a psychiatric hospital. The land had previously belonged to the Glamorgan Health Authority who ran the hospital; the Authority's initial intention had been to supply the hospital with provisions grown on the farmland.

A farm manager had been appointed but, in the event, there had been almost minimal investment in the land with the hedges and drainage being neglected for many years. The soil was unsuitable for arable farming and, with continued neglect, also proved unsuitable for stock farming.

Howard Joyce had been in a dilemma as to what to do with this land in the longer term. Some of the woods near Hensol had already been used by the Cardiff Equestrian Club for various charity events and the possibility of a full-blown equestrian centre was an option. An alternative, taking advantage of the growing leisure market in South Wales, would be the establishment of a hotel, golf course and leisure club. Architects were consulted and appropriate applications made but the Vale of Glamorgan Authority proved very negative about such a development on the site and turned down the planning application.

Howard successfully appealed to the Welsh Office against the planning refusal but this inevitably involved considerable time and expense and, as he recalls here, the services of specialist consultants:

*"I remember that one of the objections against the proposals centred on the disturbance of the second largest*

*heronry in Wales which was nearby. I consulted an ornithologist who then acted for me in the appeal hearing. One of the representatives of the local authority asked what would happen if a golf ball hit a heron on the leg as it was crossing one of the greens. The ornithologist succinctly replied 'it would be a very stupid heron'!"*

[Howard Joyce]

When approval was eventually granted by the Welsh Office Howard's original idea was to lease the land to the nearby Llantrisant and Pontyclun Golf Club. Members of that club had for many years complained about the limitations of their course which was originally nine holes but was subsequently extended by a further three holes. However, perhaps understandably, there were conflicts within the membership: some of the older members – and particularly those who lived in houses surrounding the golf course – were against such a move while younger, more aspiring golfers were attracted to the idea of playing a potentially more challenging golf course nearby. There was also the financial appeal of selling the existing Llantrisant Golf Course for housing development and various builders, notably Barratts of South Wales, were interested in working with them on such a project. However, other householders in the Talbot Green locality were also against it and understandably appalled at the possibility of further development on what they saw as the only 'green belt' area in their village.

Howard waited patiently for some two-and-a-half years for a decision from the club. However, after much soul-searching, members and committee could not agree a way forward, particularly as planning permission for residential housing on the Llantrisant course was eventually declined.

Meanwhile Peter Johnson and Ginny Golding had begun putting together their own idea for a golf course project. They contacted Howard and, on 28th May 1992, agreed to lease part of the land for five years with an option thereafter to either purchase the site or extend the lease:

*"The pioneering spirit that Ginny and I had at the beginning of the project was fantastic. I lived for some time in a caravan on the middle of what is now the . . . putting green at the front of the golf clubhouse. On very cold nights I would have to go into our first clubhouse, which was a transportable wooden shed, for a shower simply to keep warm. Anyhow, on New Year's Eve at the end of that first year, I went off to a party to celebrate [our progress]. I left my dog Goldie on guard in the caravan; unfortunately he must have knocked over an internal light and the caravan caught fire. Incredibly Goldie had the sense to lie down near an air vent and survived a most unpleasant accident. What a dog!"*

*[Peter Johnson]*

The Vale of Glamorgan planning authority once again required certain conditions to be met, particularly road widening towards the proposed entrance, before any development could continue. It was partly due to these problems over access that Peter had his first contact with Gerald, who lived nearby, and which led to the possibility being raised of the Leekes Group having some involvement in the golf project. Gerald initially was disinterested, recognising that the existing consortium simply did not have the financial resources that would be needed for the full development of such a project.

It took time and back-achingly hard graft for Peter Johnson's and Ginny Golding's project to prove its market appeal – but the hard-won success was substantial:

*"The initial greens on the nine-hole course were formed using much of the ash from the hospital itself. There must have been 70 or 80 years' worth of ash available from the old boilers and this provided an excellent drainage foundation for some of the holes. Of course this was at a time when it was very much a "do-it-yourself" project for*

*all of us. All the directors were involved in some way or another. I remember Peter Walker trying to drive the club mower and becoming bogged down on the second green. It took almost three days to retrieve the mower and, inevitably, the leg-pulling for Peter was substantial . . .*

*". . . our initial idea was to start off with a driving range and a nine-hole golf course. At the beginning of 1992 we launched a debenture scheme and although some people took up this offer, in reality response was rather limited. Subsequently, as the range and course were completed towards the end of that year, we took on some 500 members within a seven-week period."*

*[Peter Johnson]*

Naturally other investors were also being sought at the same time. Consortium member Peter Walker remembers his discussions with wealthy Cardiff property developer and entrepreneur Mike McCarthy.

*"Besides the original golf range, which was built at a cost of £70,000, we had developed the adjoining nine-hole Hensol course designed by Peter Johnson. These developments aroused fierce objection from the people with adjoining properties who challenged every proposal being made.*

*"When I showed Mike around our project he gave his potential involvement due consideration but eventually declined with the maxim – "I never invest in anything that eats or grows"!"*

*[Peter Walker]*

Despite the fact that Gerald had recently become disillusioned with his involvement in a similar but smaller sporting complex in southern Spain, his interest in the development was stimulated as it progressed. Following further discussions with Peter Johnson and Peter Walker, Leekes eventually agreed to take a 51 per cent share in the business.

To develop the new 18-hole course to the exacting standards demanded by modern-day golfers required an enormous investment, which in reality was beyond the resources of the original directors. Gerald had, however, recognised both the potential of the overall development and that, in the consortium, a good team was already in place for what would be the initial stage: Peter Johnson with his vast technical expertise in golf course design, and the redoubtable Ken Thomas, seconded from his duties with the retail stores and with his local knowledge and land management expertise, formed an excellent partnership.

United States Golf Association specification standards were obtained for the green designs and the specialist materials required were sourced locally wherever possible. Glyn Stephens Plant Hire was one of the main local contractors, and great care was taken to ensure the course design made little impact on the local ecology: in fact, over 23,000 trees were planted in conjunction with the Forestry Commission. When the new Lake Course was completed in October 1994, little did anyone expect that its popularity through increasing membership and visiting societies would place an almost impossible burden on the course's usage.

Head green keeper John Borja (left) discusses the 23,000-strong tree-planting project with Tree Scene project manager David Wilkes (Autumn 1994)

The 12th green on the Lake Course, which is completely surrounded by water

When it was just three years old the Lake Course started to attract various famous faces. In 1997, his benefit year, the Glamorgan wicketkeeper Colin Metson held various golfing events and on 22nd August the legendary West Indian cricketer Sir Garfield Sobers played the Lake Course with three guests in support of the benefit.

## Warne and pals take top prize

THE touring Australian cricketers showed off their golfing talents during their visit to Wales. They supported Colin Metson's benefit day at the Vale of Glamorgan Club by entering three teams – including the winners.

Australia's A team of Shane Warne, Ricky Ponting, Geoff Marsh and Ray Phillips (of tour spon-

WINNERS: (l-r) Colin Metson, Shane Warne, Ricky Ponting, Geoff Marsh, Peter Johnson (Vale of Glamorgan Golf Club), Ray Phillips.

sors Coca-Cola Australia) carried off first prize.

"The Aussies gave me wonderful support and showed that they are just as competitive on the golf course as they are on the cricket pitch," said Metson.

The golf day was the latest in a number of high profile events organised for the Glamorg an benficiary.

One of the highlights is the gala dinner at the Forte Posthouse, Swansea, on August 22, when Sir Garfield Sobers will be the guest speaker.

In July 1997 the touring Australian cricket team entered three golfing teams for the Colin Metson benefit, including the winners. Left to right: Colin Metson, Shane Warne, Ricky Ponting, Geoff Marsh, Peter Johnson and Ray Phillips

1997 also culminated in the staging of the PGA Wales and the West Championship on the Lake Course as part of an extremely successful three-year, £100,000 sponsorship package agreed between Leekes and the PGA.

A difficulty experienced by all new golf course developers is to obtain a return on their substantial capital investment in land and building costs. Substantial losses were incurred as competing against long-established golf clubs where these capital costs have long since been written off is extremely difficult, and making a profit is impossible without charging uncompetitively high green fees.

It became obvious to Gerald that in order to reverse those losses the leisure club and hotel would have to be built as soon as possible. The sums invested by the original shareholders now became insignificant compared to the substantial amounts which

The PGA Welsh Championship sponsorship deal is signed: (left to right) Gerald Leeke, Peter Johnson and Ray Ellis, secretary of the Wales and West region of the PGA

Stephen Leeke presents the winner's trophy to Richard Dinsdale in 1999, joined by Peter Johnson

would be involved in the ongoing development. So a meeting was held with all shareholders to discuss the proposition that all shares be purchased by the Leekes Group, and all directors' loans repaid. This was passed, with a request by the original directors to retain a small shareholding also agreed.

147

## THE LEISURE CLUB

By the mid-1990s consumer confidence was increasing enormously after the recessionary years at the beginning of the decade. The amount of time and money consumers were spending on health and leisure activities had been steadily increasing and leisure and sports businesses were benefiting as more people invested in healthier lifestyles. In South Wales, leisure clubs at hotels such as the Celtic Manor Resort in Newport, the capital's Copthorne and Marriott, and Fredericks, attached to the Miskin Manor Hotel, plus other, newer developments, such as the David Lloyd Centre off Cardiff's Newport Road, had already taken advantage of this growing market. Given the profitability of the leaders in this field it was decided that the leisure club would be built ahead of but as a complement to the future hotel.

The advice from Adrian Davies, who had visited many of the best leisure clubs throughout Europe during his squash career, was invaluable to Gerald and his team throughout this period. Together with Adrian, Gerald and Terry Jones visited a number of prestigious clubs both in the UK and mainland Europe, and began to take advice from various specialists in the field:

*"I remember that one of the best-known experts in this field was a Dutch architect. Adrian, Terry and I went across to Holland to visit some of the leisure clubs he had designed and he gave us some very useful advice. He had also told us that he was an excellent tennis player and we decided to have a game together one evening to break up the various business visits. Naturally we had no specialist tennis gear with us and turned out looking a fairly scruffy bunch. Our host, however, was simply immaculately dressed.*

*"We agreed that Terry should play with him as he was considered the weakest of our trio. Anyhow, Adrian took the first serve and hit the ball so hard that it simply shot past our host and missed his chin by inches. The whole thing happened so quickly he simply didn't have any time*

Start of work on the leisure club site in 1997

*to move. Of course he didn't know that Adrian, instead of choosing squash, could have been an international standard tennis player!"*

*[Gerald Leeke]*

A number of excellent facilities were visited, particularly in Holland and Germany, and Gerald and Terry learned a lot about leisure club design. At the same time a survey by consultants KPMG was commissioned and, while this confirmed a business case for a club, they recommended a small, select development forecasting that perhaps at best some 700 to 800 members could be anticipated. Gerald's gut feeling was that this was incorrect advice and he decided to build the biggest possible club on the site. The overall design was put together by Terry Jones with engineering help from Peter Jones of the Nicholson Jones Partnership and architectural support from Paul Larcombe:

*"In view of our involvement with squash we decided at least three squash courts were needed, but using the revolutionary concept of glass backed walls with moveable internal walls to give complete flexibility on the usage of*

149

*the courts. We also felt a large spa should be included and, with over 20 rooms, it became the largest in Wales."*

*[Gerald Leeke]*

As ever, the core building team was made up of Leekes people; Ken Thomas was site manager and Dennis Wattley site foreman. This was an enormous logistical operation for people who had no previous experience in this area, but Gerald had every confidence in the team he knew so well and preferred to have them at the core rather than recruit unknown specialists. At the same time, he ensured that expert consultants were used for each part of the project: leisure company operators Tweedpark helped in the layout design, Techno Gym advised on gym equipment, and experts from exclusive London spa The Sanctuary advised on layouts, processes and staff training for the spa element of the development which commenced in 1997.

While Gerald was leading the construction his son Stephen was charged with setting up the business, becoming managing director of the Vale Resort in 1998 alongside his role as sales director of Leekes.

The recruitment of the membership began in earnest as soon as the building work started. This was done from a small conservatory (courtesy of Leekes, of course) placed in what is now the main hotel car park. Linda Taylor headed the Leekes internal team and a specialist membership sales consultant, Rachel Browse, was employed to give advice and guidance on membership recruitment processes. The interest was phenomenal and over 2,200 members joined before the club actually opened in 1998.

*"Having rejoined Leekes, after previously being employed in the stores, I was asked to become involved in membership recruitment and little did I know that our first office was to be a conservatory in the car park! It was one of the hottest summers I can remember and the temperature was absolutely stifling in that conservatory.*

*"It seemed amazing that people were prepared to join a leisure club before anything was built. I had to explain the layout and facilities of the club to them from some drawings. It was the summer of 1998, a year before the Rugby World Cup was held in Wales, and we had flags of all the countries hung around the conservatory just to brighten things up. It was so hot during the day and then very damp in the evening, so that all the colours on the flags faded and mushrooms began to grow on the floor of our office. Despite all that it was a fantastic time. It was really exciting and one of my most enjoyable periods at work."*

*[Linda Taylor]*

The design of the club took advantage of the existing land contours and its future purpose as a complement to the hotel was taken into account. As it was being built, preparations were made for the eventual underground servicing of the hotel to be made through the basement of the club.

When the project was completed it contained three squash courts, three international-standard outdoor tennis courts, a 20-metre indoor swimming pool, three fitness and aerobic studios, a large, fully-equipped gymnasium and a specialist beauty clinic and spa, which was initially operated in conjunction with The Sanctuary. In the early days Tweedpark managed the leisure club jointly with the Leekes team.

Ron Davies MP, then Secretary of State for Wales, was invited to perform the official opening ceremony on 26th October 1998. No-one knew then that this would be his last formal engagement before what would become one of the most infamous incidents in Welsh or even UK political history. After the celebrations Gerald remembers escorting the Secretary of State to his waiting car. Mr Davies explained that he would be driving to London for political appointments the following day. It is, of course, now well known that, en route to his London appointments, the former MP for Caerphilly experienced what he famously referred

151

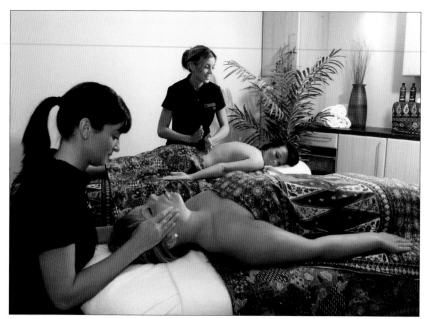

The Vale Leisure Club's luxury spa

to as his "moment of madness" on Clapham Common, which eventually led to his resignation as Secretary of State for Wales.

Gerald's gut instinct on the numbers a large leisure club would be able to attract at this location was proved to be bang on target, as Paul Beddoe testifies:

> *"When the club finally opened we already had more than 2,200 members and had to stagger the opening to accommodate the rush to visit: now we have over 5000 members."*
>
> *[Paul Beddoe]*

> *"While building the leisure club we had experienced huge problems with ground conditions. In view of the fact that the plant and the experienced contractors were already on site I decided to go ahead and build the foundations of the hotel as well and once the foundations were built, at considerable cost, it was a case of 'we might as well finish the job and complete the hotel'."*
>
> *[Gerald Leeke]*

The pool at the Vale Leisure Club

Members using the newly-opened leisure club (1998)

## THE VALE HOTEL

Prior to the detailed design of the hotel a further survey was commissioned which found that the hotel market could be divided into two distinct classifications – either in a city centre or in an out-of-town location, each of which attracted a different type of customer.

As far as local out-of-town competition was concerned, the Copthorne Hotel at Culverhouse Cross, Cardiff, on the edge of the Vale area, was found to be the major player, with 135 bedrooms. Other, smaller hotels such as the nearby Miskin Manor, the Heronston and Coed-y-Mwstwr hotels at Bridgend and St Mary's Hotel and Country Club near Pencoed offered rather more specialist facilities but with a limited number of rooms. The closest hotel to the proposed Vale development was the Miskin Manor which had been sold to private developers in 1996 after being in receivership for some three-and-a-half years. Additional competition was also on the horizon with the proposed opening of the new Village Hotel and Leisure Club at Coryton in north Cardiff.

Once again planning issues came to the fore and the Vale of Glamorgan planning authority raised a number of obstacles should the proposed hotel exceed 100 bedrooms, maintaining that a maximum of 80 bedrooms would be approved. To obtain the best return on any investment, Gerald had discovered that a hotel needed to have accommodation well in excess of that amount, to take advantage of both the economies of scale and the golf, conference and wedding markets. Eventually, by a process of wit and ingenuity, a proposal for 143 rooms was approved.

The plan at this stage was for Leekes to develop the hotel which would then be run by an established hotel operator. Paul McCarthy of Cardiff-based advertising agency Merlin, whose services had been utilised by Leekes for some time, was well aware of developments at the Vale and introduced Gerald to Donald Macdonald, the previous managing director of the Stakis Hotel Group who was then building up his chain of Macdonald hotels.

Gerald, together with Terry Jones, visited a number of hotels owned by the Macdonald chain and they were impressed by a hotel which consisted of a converted main house combined with three separate lodges, originally stables and coach houses. They believed that such a design would suit the Hensol site more than a single, large building, giving a viable number of bedrooms while satisfying the planning authorities.

> *"I remember our trip to Scotland to meet Donald Macdonald. The main part of our discussion one evening centred on whether Leekes could design and build its own hotel and subsequently run it. We ended up discussing the layout over a couple of pints in a very poorly lit bar. I remember Gerald drawing the concept on the back of a beer mat. The core idea was as simple as that. Goodness knows what happened to that beer mat, but a framed copy of it might just be worth a few quid today!"*
>
> *[Terry Jones]*

Gerald Leeke (right) discusses progress with Richard Board (left) of main contractors, Cowbridge-based Arby Construction, and Phil Rees, site manager for groundwork and construction company Blackwells of Swansea

Subsequently Gerald and Terry consolidated their ideas regarding the design and then briefed an architect to prepare detailed plans. At that stage it was still considered most likely that a hotel group would actually run the completed facility and talks were held with groups such as Thistle, Hilton, Marriot and Macdonald himself. Thistle was originally interested but eventually backed out due to financial problems, and Macdonald, whose main strengths then lay in managing basic hotels with low overheads, was considered not to be a suitable partner. It was time to accept a new challenge and become a hotel operator.

As the building work for the hotel began in earnest, the issue of recruiting key new staff members had to be addressed. The target was to open the hotel by October 1999 in order to capitalise on the interest generated by the Rugby World Cup which was being hosted by Wales with many of the most important games being held at the new Millennium Stadium in Cardiff.

First and foremost it was important to recruit an experienced hotel manager and Simon Read had been recommended to Gerald by contacts at furniture supplier Christie Tyler who frequently used the Copthorne Hotel in Cardiff. Simon had been manager between 1991 and 1996 before moving to the Copthorne Hotel at Slough. He remembered Leekes having a Christmas party one year at the Cardiff Copthorne but, other than that, knew little of the Group or its planned hotel and leisure complex.

Eventually his interest was aroused enough to attend an interview one Saturday morning in 1999 when he met Gerald and others from the Leekes team in the golf clubhouse. Simon was genuinely excited by the prospect of this new venture and eventually accepted an offer to join in the summer of 1999. But despite the initial formal interview, the laid-back Leekes style of recruitment soon re-emerged:

*"I remember at the time that we were in the process of recruiting Simon Read that a group of friends from the golf*

*club decided to go on a golfing holiday to South Africa.
You can imagine that everyone was in holiday mood and
on the way to London for the flight we stopped off at the
Hungerford junction of the M4 and had lunch in The
Pheasant pub.*

*"I had told Simon that we would be passing through that
area and, as he was still working at Slough at the time, we
arranged to meet to conclude some details. He turned up at
the pub dressed like a tailor's dummy while everyone else –
many who would be his future colleagues – were in casual
clothing and high spirits. Goodness knows what he thought
of us. I really did think that it was possible he might not
accept the offer to join us due to that meeting!"*

*[Gerald Leeke]*

"To the Vale!" Gerald (back right) drinks a toast to the hotel at its topping out ceremony with site agent Richard Board and, front left, Stephen Leeke, Vale managing director and, right, Simon Read, Vale general manager (summer 1999)

But accept he did and, while working out the remainder of his contract with the Copthorne Group, Simon would travel down to the Hensol complex on Saturday mornings to keep in touch with progress and offer practical and technical advice in relation to the hotel's design.

Simon's contacts within the hotel trade ensured that the initial team was substantially based around his previous Copthorne colleagues. These included head chef Mark Jameson, food and beverage manager Melanie Hancock, head concierge Tony Viggers, maintenance manager Paul Skinner, food and beverage controller Julian Baker, personnel manager Nick Edwards, sous chef Wayne Tapscott, sales manager Tracey Evans and events manager Darren Hubbard. Many of these would stay with the new project for several years and did much to ensure its immediate success.

The hotel opened for business in time for the Rugby World Cup in October 1999 although, despite the best efforts of everyone – including Gerald who would be seen sweeping out newly-finished hotel rooms – only 28 bedrooms were actually ready and available for World Cup visitors. However, the restaurants, bar and reception rooms were and around 450 people used the hotel for pre- and post-match hospitality on the day of the Final. The main guests of honour on that occasion were Archbishop Desmond Tutu and Brian Moore, the former England rugby hooker: the contrast between one of Africa's most famous religious icons and England's well-known "pitbull" must have been something to savour.

Simon Read recalls the first few months after opening when any bookings were welcome – well, almost:

> *"During the early months of the hotel opening we were prepared to take any visitors. On one occasion we had a wedding party staying here and the bride and groom had their pet dog as their guest-of-honour. After the reception the dog was placed back in their room but created havoc*

*howling and crying and keeping others in adjoining rooms awake. We offered to relocate other guests but it was impossible. In those days we might have accepted a kangaroo or a llama as a pet in the hotel but now we are much more fussy."*

[Simon Read]

The hotel was fitted out to the highest standards. Contacts through the Leekes stores with manufacturers both in the UK and in the Far East helped enormously to reduce the fitting-out costs and attention-to-detail was second-to-none to ensure guests' satisfaction.

The hotel was officially opened by Rhodri Morgan MP, First Minister of the National Assembly for Wales, in June 2000. It quickly earned a reputation as being the venue of choice for everything from weddings to accommodation for national and international sporting teams to business conferences. It also quickly became the choice of world famous stars – most of whom Simon Read and his team could accommodate:

*"One of the most famous pop groups perhaps was Westlife. They were all very keen golfers and all had new sets of golf clubs provided prior to their arrival at the hotel. They were certainly excellent customers in our golf shop.*

*"We must be one of the few hotels ever to have turned down a reservation from Elton John. He was performing one of his amazing concerts at Margam Park near Port Talbot and his manager was interested in reserving the honeymoon suite at the hotel. The only problem was that he wanted the room completely redecorated in an unusual yellow colour. It would have been marvellous to have had him staying here but we were regrettably forced to turn him down."*

[Simon Read]

The rear of the hotel with the 18th green in the foreground and showing the Lakes Restaurant, housed in a large, Victorian conservatory

The front of the hotel after dark

The Resort developed considerably and quickly as soon as it opened, and has proved an enormous success story, with occupancy rates reaching 90 per cent – one of the highest in Wales. One of its most significant additions in 2001 was the hotel's Lakes Restaurant – a large Victorian conservatory seating up to 200 diners – whose superb setting overlooks the eponymous golf course. The latest, significant addition, Mediterranean-style restaurant La Cucina, opened in autumn 2005 to cater for local diners as well as offer guests an alternative to the hotel's main restaurant.

La Cucina

Aerial view of the Vale Resort, with the Lesiure Club in the foreground and the Hotel and Lodges behind

In November 2006 the Vale welcomed world-famous novelist Jilly Cooper whose many bestsellers include *Rivals*, *Riders* and *Polo*. Jilly was guest-of-honour at an exclusive luncheon held at the hotel in aid of NSPCC Cymru/Wales to launch her latest novel, *Wicked*. The hero of the book is an ex-Wales international rugby star and Jilly had spent many an hour at the Resort soaking up the atmosphere of the Welsh team in training before writing the important chapter in the book where the hero and heroine finally "get together" in the Vale Resort's Indoor Arena.

Jilly Cooper at the Vale Hotel, November 2006

# Chapter 11

# BUILDING A SPORTING REPUTATION

## DEVELOPMENT OF THE INDOOR ARENA

The Vale's popularity with the UK's sporting elite is now well-known, with Premier League teams literally arguing over who is to stay at the hotel way ahead of cup finals or other fixtures at Cardiff's Millennium Stadium. But, largely as a result of Simon Read's influence and contacts, right from its opening the Wales rugby team had chosen to stay at the Vale Hotel in the weeks prior to major international matches, and its attraction soon spread, boosted by the development of an indoor training facility:

> *"From the very beginning we had a good relationship with the Welsh Rugby Union and the Football Association of Wales. Apart from those bodies we have hosted many football teams including Arsenal, Liverpool, Blackburn, Manchester United, Lazio and Wolves with rugby visitors including Munster, Leinster, Newcastle and the British Lions. Naturally the construction of the training "barn" at the top end of our main car park provided a huge advantage."*
>
> *[Simon Read]*

Gerald's vision of the Vale becoming a centre for sporting excellence was taking shape – and his development of the indoor training arena was a major factor. But how did it come about? The seed was planted soon after the hotel opened in 2000 when Gerald was having a drink with then Wales rugby team coach Graham Henry.

Henry and team manager David Pickering were then using Pencoed College's Equestrian Training Centre for indoor training with the team in inclement weather. Graham talked to Gerald about the indoor training facilities used back in his native New Zealand: a disused aircraft hangar, which contained a pitch whose earth surface had to be regularly watered to keep the dust down. He said that, while such training barns worked well, the surface was not ideal: Gerald was sure the Leekes team could go one better and Adrian Davies was no stranger to his can-do attitude:

> *"I remember talking with Gerald and Graham Henry in the bar at the hotel and Graham was moaning about the fact that they had no indoor training facilities in Wales. Having listened for some time Gerald said 'We'll build you one!'. He then turned to me and said 'Off you go – and find a better surface!'."*
>
> *[Adrian Davies]*

At the time there was a powerful lobby within the Welsh Rugby Union (WRU) to locate its training centre in Gwent. Peter Walker's strong presentation skills, developed while running his company, Merlin Television Ltd, would be invaluable when he and Vale managing director Stephen Leeke made a presentation to the Executive Committee of the WRU on the advantages of basing the centre at the Vale Resort. According to WRU insiders that presentation won over many of the doubters and supporters of the Gwent location. It certainly helped pave the way for the ongoing good relationship with the WRU and subsequently with other sports bodies, particularly the Football Association of Wales (FAW).

A covered area at least half the size of a full playing pitch was required with, of course, considerable height specifications. Their research for the training barn was both thorough and exciting:

> *"As part of the planning for the indoor training arena we were introduced by Mark Hughes, the Wales football*

*manager who was regularly based at the Resort, to Sir Alex Ferguson, manager of Man United. Gerald, Terry and I then visited Carrington, United's training ground and Sir Alex showed us around. It was amazing. All the stars were there – Beckham, Giggs, Keane and so on – and the level of professionalism in the overall set-up was overwhelming. I also got on well with Beckham's son Brooklyn who was there and must have been about two. Gerald suggested that it must have been due to having similar interests!"*

*[Adrian Davies]*

The playing surface needed to be better than some of the options then available on the UK market: Astra turf – which has been used at a range of internal training venues for many years – could create problems with skin abrasions. So Adrian began researching alternatives and came up with a final recommendation for a surface called "field turf" which was being used in American Football. This rubber-backed carpet with a variety of texture options would be used for the first time in the UK at the Vale's indoor training arena and was suitable for use in contact sports.

As work on the building began negotiations with the WRU unfortunately became somewhat fraught. Under its old committee structure the WRU had gained an unenviable reputation for equivocation on almost every issue and this occasion was no different. Yet, despite some initial difficulties, agreement was eventually reached on the basis of a joint venture company with a 50/50 use of the facility. So when the WRU was not using the indoor arena the Vale Resort could make the facility available to other clubs and organisations who had expressed an interest.

Once again the success of the venture brought its own challenges. Leekes' sponsorship of Cardiff City Football Club in the 2002/2003 season progressed into an arrangement for the club to use the arena as their soccer academy. In addition the

FAW was also using the hotel as its preferred venue prior to matches and naturally wished to use what it saw as a superb facility. Suddenly the arena was in much higher demand and expansion was necessary!

The Welsh Rugby Union gym at the Vale indoor arena

The finishing touches are put to the special playing surface at the Vale's indoor arena

All sorts of alternatives and other locations were examined but eventually it was agreed that an extension to the existing arena was the best option and it was completed at the end of 2003. The FAW Trust, which is responsible for junior football in Wales, moved into the front end of the arena in March 2004 with the WRU relocating to a new, improved facility at the rear.

Apart from the indoor training facility itself the arena now houses various offices, a gymnasium and a sports science section, all of which are available for the administrators of and participants in Wales's two major sports. With both the national rugby and football teams firmly located at the Vale Resort it had now become a true multi-sport location favoured by the highest profile sportsmen in Wales. The achievement of Gerald's vision has been succinctly confirmed by Sir Clive Woodward:

*"The indoor arena was built within six months but has developed and improved from its early beginnings. It was especially pleasing when Sir Clive Woodward, the hugely*

Captain Ryan Giggs and the Wales squad training at the Indoor Arena

*successful rugby coach of England when they won the World Cup, visited the unit during 2005 and declared the facilities 'state-of-the-art, fantastic and the best in the world'. When he was appointed as their coach he was impressed enough to base the British Lions squad at the Vale Resort for a week prior to their 2005 tour of New Zealand. His view seems to have been endorsed by others, notably the New Zealand and Australian coaches who have been based there while coaching Wales and who felt that, in this almost hidden part of South Wales, we have something that is equal to anything in the world."*

*[Gerald Leeke]*

The Vale also enjoyed a five-year reputation in the highest sporting circles as 'the lucky hotel' with Premiership football clubs fighting to make it their base. It all began in 2001 when the FA Cup Final was played at the Millennium Stadium for the first time while Wembley was being rebuilt. The Resort first earned the tag after Liverpool supremo Michael Owen grabbed two late goals for his team in the last eight minutes to sink Arsenal: his team were staying at the Vale.

Since that day superstitious sports stars have battled almost as hard as they do on the pitch to stay at the hotel – and have been rewarded with victory almost every time. The mighty Arsenal, still smarting after their late defeat in 2001, fought off stiff competition from Chelsea in 2002 and Southampton in 2003 to bag rooms at 'the Lucky Vale' and collected winners' medals both times. In 2006 Vale Resort mania reached new heights when desperate football fans were caught up in an eBay bidding frenzy that ended with over £1000 being paid for a sought-after double room alongside FA Cup finalists West Ham. Just when we thought it was all over and the Vale's lucky record would remain intact the final FA Cup Final was played in Cardiff before its return to Wembley – and West Ham were beaten on penalties by Liverpool.

Steven Gerrard, Simon Read, Sami Hypia and Michael Owen celebrate at the Vale

And the luck was not just confined to guests staying at the hotel. In August 2003 three of the players competing in the WPGA Ladies Championship of Europe at Royal Porthcawl Golf Club and staying at the Vale were taking a look around the Lake Course. As they approached the tee of the par three tenth hole Gerald and three friends – Terry Jones, Paul Beddoe and Lyndon Thomas – were about to tee off. Gerald, who had already met the lady competitors during the tournament's pro-am and was always up for a contest, challenged them to see if they could beat his team 'at nearest to the pin'. After taking off their shoes and borrowing a club all three ladies put their balls within 15 feet of the hole. While Lyndon, Terry and Paul all failed to match their shots, Gerald played a shot which landed just short of the green and rolled in for his first hole-in-one!

## The development of the Wales National Course

The old saying "necessity is the mother of invention" is particularly apt with regard to the development of the Wales National Course at the Vale Resort, which began as the 20th century drew to a close.

The Resort's success, with high occupancy rates at the hotel, particularly from golf societies and other keen golfers, put huge pressure on both the Lake and its adjoining nine-hole course. It had become obvious that to retain the advantages of a full and active membership and to exploit fully the commercial opportunities from visiting golfers from all over the world, a second 18-hole course was needed, built to the highest international standards.

The possibility of the 2010 Ryder Cup coming to the Celtic Manor Resort, just 15 miles up the M4, concentrated the minds of Gerald, Steve and their marketing department, headed up by Paul Beddoe.

With two top-class championship courses and a high quality hotel The Vale Resort would be an attractive venue in this period – and beyond – to golf fans from the USA in particular. There was a clear and considerable commercial advantage in extending the existing nine-hole course by a further nine holes, and the opportunity arose when Duffryn Llof Farm, next to the Vale, was put up for sale.

After the purchase of this 90-acre farm, 15 acres of additional land adjacent to the road that now runs through the National Course were purchased from Wally Abbot, who owned a smallholding near the new development.

Since the development of the Lake Course the Leekes team had visited a number of golfing complexes overseas and throughout the UK and were particularly impressed by the appearance and attention-to-detail of Druids Glen Golf Club, south of Dublin. They decided that a similar landscaping design would add to the attraction of the new National Course.

The Wales National Course showing the fairways of the 15th and 13th holes with the 16th green in the foreground

Peter Johnson took the lead in preparing an outline plan for the new course, but planning problems relating to almost every aspect of the proposed development were immediately raised by the Vale of Glamorgan Council during a preparatory meeting. With the Vale of Glamorgan Unitary Development Plan favouring tourism ventures which both assisted local economic development and safeguarded and enhanced the environment, no-one could have foreseen the complex difficulties of making the project – which fulfilled both objectives – actually happen.

After the initial rejection of the proposals, planning and environmental consultants Chapman Warren were engaged to assess the impact of the development on an endless range of protected species of birds, animals and plants which lived on the land earmarked for development.

This area was hugely rich in wildlife: it was both home to certain protected species and a fertile breeding ground – with 53 species of birds alone choosing to breed here. The effects of development on the resident mammals, including badgers, moles, water shrews and colonies of tree bats, would need to be considered with extreme care. The Leekes team suddenly had to become familiar with the breeding eccentricities of wonderfully named birds such as the nightjar, reed warbler, sprawk and lesser whitethroat. Various specialist nature groups and the Countryside Council for Wales all had an active interest in ensuring that every care would be taken to avoid damaging indigenous habitats.

The task seemed enormous but, fortunately, the Wales Tourist Board was extremely supportive and a suitably encouraged Gerald advised the local authority that he intended appealing against any adverse planning decision, which would result in considerable litigation costs. Fortunately good sense eventually prevailed and the planning application, when submitted, was approved, but not without an extensive range of conditions.

And so another challenging project for the Leekes team began towards the end of the year 2000: constructing the new National

Sir Steve Redgrave with many other well-known sports personalities in one of his Golden Five events held to launch the opening of the National Course in June 2003

Course, which endeavoured to achieve the magical figure of 7,500 yards in length in order to become one of the longest outside the USA. It was designed to hold a particular challenge for the professional and low-handicap golfers while still appealing to the average enthusiast – and with the intention of attracting some major competitions in the future.

During the construction phase, the complete rearrangement of the old nine-hole course and its temporary closure inevitably put further pressure on the already overused Lake Course. But, eventually, the National Course, the newest addition to the Vale Hotel, Golf and Spa Resort, was formally opened in June 2003 by Sir Steve Redgrave, five-times rowing Olympic gold medallist and no mean golfer to boot.

While June 2003 saw the opening of the National Course it was also the month when the Leeke family held its own celebration at the hotel. This was for the 90th birthday of Mrs Myra Leeke and included a presentation entitled 'This is Your Life' by eldest son David.

Mrs Myra Leeke celebrates her 90th birthday at the Vale with her four children (left to right) David, Gerald, Diane and Stuart

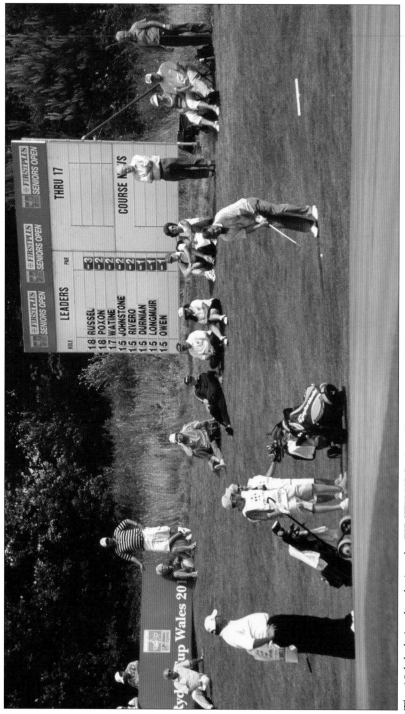

The 18th hole in play during the FIRSTPLUS Seniors Open in June 2006

The National Course has already been used for a number of major competitions as well as corporate events, and the realisation of its ambition to become one of the major locations on the European golf circuit is well underway. In 2005 the Vale hosted the European Tour Firstplus Challenge event for up-and-coming professionals and has been awarded the same tournament for 2007; in 2006 it hosted the Firstplus Wales Seniors Open for the first time, after it had been held at Royal St David's in Harlech for five successful years, attracting a stronger field and bigger galleries than ever before. An exciting finish saw Jose Rivero of Spain birdie the last hole to win the tournament along with a cheque for £75,000. Rivero, a former Ryder Cup player, finished just one shot ahead of Sam Torrance, Europe's victorious Ryder Cup Captain, and three other players.

Jose Rivero being presented with the trophy by Stephen Leeke, managing director of the Vale and Jeremy Masding of Firstplus

# Chapter 12

# STORMING THE CASTLE

On 17th December 2003 the *Western Mail* carried an article headed *"Gerald – King of the Castle"*.

The article went on to explain that the Leekes Group had successfully completed one of the most intriguing property and land deals in Wales – the acquisition of the 17th century Hensol Castle and its surrounding 150 acres of countryside.

Left to right: Gareth Roberts of Welsh Health Estates and Stephen Wade of Bro Morgannwg NHS Trust hand over the keys of the castle to Stephen and Gerald

It went on to explain that the Group had contracted to buy, for a figure believed to be in excess of £5 million, the Grade I-listed stately home that stood alongside the Vale Resort. This included the historically important mid-18th century landscaped

Hensol Park, a 15-acre lake and serpentine pond together with a large number of buildings formerly used as part of the hospital. Leekes had now begun what was probably the most exciting and challenging project in its 100-year history.

It is worth summarising here a little of the history of Hensol Castle, which has been well-documented by local historians over the years.

The original Welsh building on the site was called by various names: "Hen Starle", "Hen Ystafell" and "Hen Sail". The house became the county seat of the Jenkins family in 1672 whose head, David Jenkins, was a Justice of the Western Circuit of Wales and a supporter of Charles I during the Civil War. The property passed through his heirs until his great-granddaughter married into the Talbot family.

Charles Talbot was a lawyer who became Solicitor General and then Lord Chancellor. As a peer he took the title Baron Talbot of Hensol and was later made Earl of Shrewsbury. It was during his residency that the castle was extended to its present form, the work being completed in 1770.

The castle passed briefly into the Dynevor family and eventually to the agricultural pioneer Samuel Richardson at the turn of the 18th century. Richardson improved the estate during his tenure and it was at this time that the lakes at Hensol were added.

Benjamin Hall II, the eldest son of Dr Benjamin Hall, Chancellor of Llandaff, took ownership of the castle briefly between 1815 and 1817. It was his son, Sir Benjamin Hall, who became president of the Board of Health then the First Commissioner of Works during Prime Minister Palmerston's administration. London's world-famous Big Ben bell was cast during his period of office and named after him, and a minor version of the Big Ben clock is sited above one of the main entrances to the castle.

During the mid-19th century the castle passed through the ownership of two families of ironmasters: first the Crawshays of

Aerial view of Hensol Castle. The Vale Hotel can be seen at the top left of the picture

Cyfarthfa and then the Fothergills of Abernant. Subsequently the estate passed, through marriage, into the Price family at the start of the 20th century and in 1918 the estate was inherited by Sir Francis Rose Price. Due to heavy taxation problems he was eventually forced to sell the castle and estate to Glamorgan County Council in 1926 for £36,500. Before he left the area for Gloucester a presentation was held for Sir Francis and Lady Price at the nearby Pendoylan School where he was presented with a silver cigar case and she with a tortoiseshell toilet seat!

The castle was used by the local authority as a psychiatric hospital and, when additional blocks were built between 1935 and1955, the castle itself became an administrative base. In 1958 part of the farmland adjoining the estate was sold by order of the Ministry of Health, although the hospital still retained the farm and gardens near the castle.

During the 1990s the treatment philosophy for patients with mental illness changed completely and supported resettlement into the community, rather than being housed in hospitals, as the aim for the majority. The hospital, which at one stage accommodated 1,500 patients, was now treating a few hundred. As a result the Bro Morgannwg Trust, which was managing the estate for the National Assembly for Wales, decided to sell the property and issued an invitation to tender for interested parties to acquire the property and the land in November 2001.

The tender process became very lengthy, partly due to the problems facing the National Assembly in actually describing in detail what they were selling; the tender included so many easements and covenants regarding some of the buildings and so many unusual practices regarding utilities provision for surrounding properties that the whole purchase process became complicated and protracted.

Leekes, as an adjacent landowner through its ownership of the Vale Resort, was made aware of the potential sale. Barrie Melhuish, managing director of house builders Barratt Homes in South Wales, stimulated the interest of Gerald and his fellow directors with a proposal for a joint development. In the event, the possibility of planning permission for residential development was found to be remote so, inevitably, Barratts' interest waned.

Leekes prepared and submitted an initial outline bid but interest in the sale subsequently accelerated when rumours began to circulate throughout South Wales of a proposal from the Government to use the facilities as accommodation for asylum-seekers.

Subsequently Gerald and his team submitted a more detailed bid which included additional payments in the form of overages – sums to be paid to the local authority in recognition of the increased value of the site if future planning permissions were granted.

Finally, two years after the initial bids had been submitted, Leekes representatives were interviewed and then short-listed. All short-listed candidates were then invited to re-bid on the basis of further information provided at that stage.

Eventually Leekes was chosen on the basis of both the best price offered and the most appropriate bid received. From the first advertisement in 2001 contracts were eventually exchanged in September 2003 with completion taking place in March 2004.

Sadly March 2004 was also the month when Mrs Myra Leeke passed away in her sleep, aged 90. Although still living at her home in Groesfaen, she had been unwell for over two years following a fall. Despite needing 24-hour care during this period she had remained remarkably cheerful and, of course, maintained her interest in the business.

A private, family-only cremation took place, followed by a thanksgiving service at Llandaff Cathedral attended by over 500 people. The service was conducted by Canon Graham Holcombe who had been her vicar for many years at St David's Church, Groesfaen, where Mrs Leeke was a faithful member and former churchwarden. David read the lesson, his daughter Charlotte played 'Ar Hyd y Nos' on the French horn and Gerald's daughters Emma and Joanna read.

Window at St David's Church, Groesfaen, to mark the work of Mrs Myra Leeke as church warden

After the death of Llew Leeke, Myra had remained in close touch with the business, carrying out her husband's wish to keep a watchful eye on it in his absence. On weekdays she was delighted to prepare breakfast for Gerald and lunch for Stuart, often going back to the Llantrisant store with him for the afternoon. She could often be seen keeping an eye on the cashiers at the tills and would also walk around the store and soon informed staff members if there was anything of which she disapproved.

For almost 70 years Mrs Myra Leeke played an important role in the success of the Leekes business, and saw it grow from a humble, one-room ironmonger's shop to a multi-million-pound concern employing more than 1200 people. She had started behind the counter in the front room shop of her first family home in Court Street and went on to become company secretary and then chairman of the Leekes Retail and Leisure Group.

185

As Mrs Leeke would have expected, the Leeke family now has another significant expansion on its hands. After protracted negotiations and discussions it was time for action and the team's ideas for the redevelopment of Hensol Castle and its adjoining land had to be finalised and turned into firm proposals.

By then an old hand at making complex planning applications, Gerald now had to build on his past experiences of development to endeavour to make this most prestigious of projects happen:

> *"As part of the planning process the authorities required an environmental statement to cover the whole project. This required surveys on subjects such as landscape, ecology, archaeology, transport, noise and so on. Discussions with the planning authorities, CADW and a range of other interested bodies naturally raised concerns over parts of the development, notably the residential conversions, and satisfying them extended the decision-making process even further."*
>
> *[Gerald Leeke]*

Three elements had been incorporated into the plans which were submitted in January 2005 and finally approved in December 2006 – subject to many conditions – with work starting on site in summer 2007, three years after the purchase had been completed.

In Gerald's own words, the castle is the "jewel in the crown" at Hensol Park and the vision for this was always clear, with five-star luxury at the heart of it. Hensol Castle is to become Wales's first destination residential and day spa, with its architecturally important principal rooms serving a mixture of uses including a library, general relaxation, executive dining and a bar. Other rooms will be converted into luxury bedroom suites including adjoining dining or sitting rooms.

The clock tower entrance to its outer courtyard will become the main entrance with the courtyard itself being used as the site of a restaurant surrounded by landscaped gardens.

The new extension to the castle will house the main spa

facilities and include two swimming pools, changing rooms, a fully equipped gym and a number of medical, physiotherapy and recuperating treatment rooms. The walled garden, which used to provide produce for the house while it was being used as a residence and later for the hospital kitchens, will be fully restored to its former glory and again used to grow fresh fruit, herbs and vegetables for use by the hotel restaurants.

The second element of the plans is the on-site development of staff accommodation. The Vale's rural setting and the late hours of the hospitality industry mean that staff can often find it difficult to commute and the offer of on-site accommodation will vastly assist in the recruitment of top quality staff.

The final element of the development will be the conversion of the former wards and concert hall into luxury executive houses, fully serviced by the Vale Hotel and forming part of a gated community. Sited in the fully landscaped and maintained grounds of Hensol Park and with all the adjacent facilities of golf, health and fitness clubs and spas, together with the restaurants and other attractions of the Vale and Castle hotels, the development has already attracted interest from far and wide.

From a planning point-of-view, this was the most contentious element but from a financial point-of-view, the most critical:

> *"With the costs of the castle restoration and conversion into a destination spa in excess of £20 million, without permission for the residential element the whole scheme could not go ahead. Fortunately the principle of giving residential permissions in order to safeguard the future of a listed building had recently been accepted by the Vale Council with the redevelopment of Sully Hospital, so needless to say we used that example in our negotiations."*
>
> [Gerald Leeke]

As these activities progress the Leekes team will no doubt once again learn new skills and develop knowledge in areas they would not previously have imagined. And it would appear that the hard-working Leekes spirit is already alive and swimming in the lake!

> *"Part of the requirements of all our planning applications for Hensol prompted us to understand more about environmental issues. One day a visitor arrived at the castle explaining that he was a nationally-known expert on the habitats of otters and wanted permission to carry out a survey. Apparently the male otters in the lake could have a domain covering some 30 miles. They would typically have five or six female "acquaintances" together with their families throughout their area and visit all of them on a regular basis. I couldn't help thinking that they must be busy chaps: they ought to be working for Leekes!"*
>
> *[Gerald Leeke]*

Maybe an otter should be adopted as the Leekes team insignia. With the possible development of another retail store in the next two years, as well as the £50 million development at Hensol, there will inevitably be challenges – but we can safely predict that no-one will become bored. The team itself will, of course, be expanded as the activities at Hensol will probably mean the employment of about another 300 people.

> *"Gerald and his elder son Stephen are in the process of creating a legacy of which they, and Wales, can be justifiably proud."*
>
> *[Peter Walker]*

At the time of publication of this "Ironmonger's Tale" the ironmongers have certainly stormed the castle! The company – one of the most successful in Wales in terms of longevity, growth and diversification – is very different from those early days in Court Street a century ago.

And the wider world has been becoming increasingly aware of Gerald's achievements as eldest daughter Emma recalls:

> *"Just before Christmas 2005 my father told us he had received a letter from 10 Downing Street asking if he would accept if he were offered an honour in the New Year's Honours list. His first reaction had been one of disbelief and his first thought was that this was the latest of Adrian Davies's elaborate wind-ups!"*
>
> *[Emma Leeke]*

Finally convinced of its authenticity, he accepted and in January 2006 received official confirmation that he had been awarded the OBE *"for services to the retail and leisure industries and to the community in South Wales"*. This was closely followed by a letter inviting him to attend Buckingham Palace to receive his OBE. But there was a problem, as Emma Leeke reveals:

> *"Dad was invited to take along three guests – trouble is, we're a family of six and we four children naturally all wanted to go along with our parents. Loads of methods of selection of two out of us were discussed and finally we put our names into a hat. Luckily for me we girls got lucky and so my sister Joanna and I looked forward to our day at the Palace!*
>
> *"My father announced his honour to the business in his typically self-deprecating style with a memo to all staff. It said that he had been awarded this OBE on the back of "others' bloody efforts" and that he was most grateful to all staff, past and present, for their contribution to the success of the business."*
>
> *[Emma Leeke]*

On 26th May 2006 Sue, Emma and Joanna proudly watched Gerald receive his OBE from Prince Charles:

*"We had tears running down our faces – it was a great day.
Our brothers then joined us for a celebratory meal at the
River Café and we headed home for Dad's surprise party at
the Vale Golf Club with family and friends."*

[Emma Leeke]

First the Castle, now the Palace: Gerald with his OBE at Buckingham Palace,
joined by, from left, daughter Joanna, wife Sue and elder daughter Emma

*Chapter 13*

# SAME SPIRIT, NEW GENERATION

Listening to the newest generation of the Leeke family to join the business is an astonishing experience. They talk enthusiastically about their heritage, each other, their vision for their family business and, most particularly, their father. The bitter rivalries and carefully rehearsed words most commonly associated with family businesses couldn't be further from the warm, unrestrained, laughter-ridden banter between four people who are increasingly carrying the Leekes business forward.

All high achievers with various university degrees (but each one majored in business), Emma, Stephen, Joanna and Christopher Leeke unanimously agree that it's "great" working for their family business – "no downsides at all". In the words of the Leekes Group's financial director Mike Fowler:

> *"It's absolutely remarkable that a family of four people who get on so well can also contribute to the business in the ways and to the level that they do."*
>
> *[Mike Fowler]*

You could be forgiven for thinking that these four driven and focussed individuals had been groomed from a young age to take over the reins, yet they never felt particularly pushed in this direction.

*"None of us ever felt any pressure or even direction towards the business – or away from it either,"* says Stephen, now managing director of the Vale Resort.

At the same time, according to Leekes business manager Joanna and commercial director Emma, the family genes were ever-present.

191

*"Dad has given us inherent competitiveness, and a huge drive to achieve which means he has never needed to push us."*

[Joanna Littlejohn]

*"We are all desperately competitive at every level – people always laugh at the way we play board games on Christmas afternoon."*

[Emma Leeke]

However, with the total commitment of their parents to expanding the business, they had all been involved from an early age. Just like their father they all remember early Saturday or summer jobs, earning 10p a day stacking paint in Tonypandy for their grandfather, working on the (then manual) stocktake at Llantrisant every summer or helping out with the delivery of builders supplies or in the warehouse. Being the boss's son was never a privilege, as youngest son Chris was to find out when he worked at the Vale site and was gleefully given the unenviable responsibility for cleaning out the unplumbed toilet used by the contractors and for any miscellaneous "drainage" problems.

Elder daughter Emma was particularly conscious of the stores' expansion, remembering Tonypandy as well as the opening of Llantrisant, Cross Hands and Melksham stores – and she felt retail was in her blood. After ten years with Marks & Spencer she admits the size of the Leekes Group only really hit home on her first day in work in the summer of 2001.

*"Unlike the others, I always thought I'd join the business – but I had a definite plan and wanted to do my own thing first. I had travelled, got married, started my family and spent ten years learning a lot about retailing with M & S and the time was right to come home. But when I walked into the head office at Mwyndy and saw the size of the operation – in particular our customer care call centre – I had to take a deep breath."*

[Emma Leeke]

According to his children Gerald worked long hours, six days a week, always taking Sunday off – that is until trading laws were relaxed and Sunday became the second busiest retail day of the week. Just as with past generations, the young Leeke children spent time with their grandparents on a Saturday as Gerald and Sue both put the hours in. But he always made time for summer family holidays – although these and any other type of family outing would be run as efficiently as his businesses.

> *"Dad cannot bear to waste any time at all and travel was like a military operation. We all had to be ready and in the car by a precise time; if we were going by 'plane he wouldn't board until the last call and we would rarely be allowed to take anything beyond hand luggage so we wouldn't have to wait the other end. Once we got there we had to wait for any extra luggage while he arranged car hire and waited impatiently for us outside."*
>
> *[Joanna Littlejohn]*

All four children talk with pride and affection about their father and his achievements and agree that you cannot separate the man from the businessman. His hands-on approach which has characterised every business opportunity he has pursued is first on their list, and they reveal that he still opens all the correspondence for the business before it is distributed.

> *"People might think he is controlling but he hates meetings and this is his way of knowing what is going on – he sees any complaint first, for example. He can't bear to be in meetings for more than half-an-hour and never has them in his office so he can make his excuses and leave. But his knowledge of how everything in the business works is immense yet he has no problem delegating responsibility and doesn't interfere. Plus, he is very soft-hearted and empathetic, and incredibly generous."*
>
> *[Emma Leeke]*

193

She remembers a childhood trip to a local fair which defines her father's firm belief in fair play in work and outside.

> *"I won a goldfish by throwing three darts. The stallholder tried to change the rules so he didn't have to give me my prize but my dad was having none of it. It started to get a bit nasty as the fairground staff backed up their colleague, but lots of Leekes staff were there cheering on my dad as he insisted I'd won fair and square – he just would not let it go. Suffice to say I got my goldfish!"*
>
> *[Emma Leeke]*

According to Stephen, Gerald's commercial acumen translates into a personal love of a bargain, legendary within the family circle.

> *"He'll negotiate for anything: we could be in the Far East on a buying trip and he'll negotiate over a cheap, souvenir T-shirt and get a real kick out of knocking 20p off the price – and then tip the seller twice the price anyway."*
>
> *[Stephen Leeke]*

As the four chat animatedly about future expansion plans for both the retail and the leisure businesses they are optimistic and excited about the future. Apparently, this, too, is genetic . . .

> *"Our father is so positive – he absolutely believes things will turn out well. He genuinely believes, even when things are looking extremely challenging, that everyone will come round to his way of thinking – not in an autocratic way, but a 'taking people with him' kind of way. And it invariably works!"*
>
> *[Emma Leeke]*

But surely the most confident businessman has his darker moments when it all becomes a bit too much?

*"If he ever has any doubts nobody would ever know – he wouldn't admit it to a soul. He focuses away from the risk, believes it is up to you to make it happen – and makes it happen."*

[Stephen Leeke]

Unsurprisingly, according to Stephen, Gerald's biggest single achievement has to be the Vale.

*"The feasibility study recommended we open a health club for 800 members and we had 2,200 signed up before we opened. To spend £20-£25 million on a project like that could have been a disaster, but Dad had the vision to do it – and I think that's fantastic."*

[Stephen Leeke]

Members of the Leeke family involved in the business: from left, standing, Christopher Leeke, project manager, Group MD and Chairman Gerald Leeke, Stuart Leeke (Director and Company Secretary), Commercial Director Emma Leeke, MD of the Vale Resort Stephen Leeke, Joanna Littlejohn (nee Leeke), business manager, and, front, Diane Cook (nee Leeke, Director). Since this photograph was taken Matthew Leeke, son of Stuart, has also joined the Leekes family business as e-commerce distribution manager

195

So what of the future? Emma, Stephen and Joanna all have young children who they say will be left to make up their own minds about joining the family business, just as they were. But all four of Gerald's children are adamant that the Leekes empire will remain a resolutely family concern, with major expansion at the forefront of their plans: a new Leekes store within five years, expansion into e-commerce plus the development of Hensol Castle and the training academy at the Vale Resort.

Like all good tales it's probably appropriate that we reserve the option of some much later chapters with the postscript "to be continued"!

# POSTSCRIPT

# Reflections of a Rhondda Ironmonger

When I read through the draft of this story of our family business it brought home to me the extent of what has been achieved together over the last 100 years or so. During the 40 years that I have been involved I never really sat back and reflected on where we have come from – nor, for that matter, where we are going. I've always believed that the ability to react quickly to opportunities and changing circumstances helps a great deal as does luck and an inclination to believe that the glass is not half-empty but half-full – I've never been able to work out which is the most important!

Naturally there has been an incredible amount of hard work; but I'm aware that I've been fortunate to have had a grandfather who had the foresight to move from a quiet agricultural neighbourhood to set up a business in the frantic surroundings of the Rhondda Valley in the early 1900s. My parents always gave me every encouragement once I had joined the company, even with what they probably felt were risky moves at the time, and my father has probably been the biggest influence on my business career. His self-taught business skills, his ability to appreciate a fresh opportunity and then, through hard work and commitment, to carry it through, set an example I've never forgotten. I've also had the continual support and hard work from my wife Sue who, with the help of her parents, Dilwyn and Betty, managed to juggle the task of bringing up four children with her many responsibilities during the expansion of the business and has even, since her retirement, managed to bring her golf handicap down to single figures!

I must also pay tribute to the other members of the family who have contributed greatly to the success of the company.

Brother David, although not directly involved, has always made himself available for specialist advice and sister Diane, brother-in-law Alan and brother Stuart have always shown total commitment; without their loyal support the company would certainly not be where it is today.

Of all the changes and expansions we have made together in the last 40 years, I suppose the early move to Llantrisant from Tonypandy was the biggest challenge: the first steps are usually the biggest. Even now I remember looking at the huge, empty warehouse and thinking, "How on Earth are we going to fill this?"

Naturally every subsequent move has had its own particular challenges. The cultural differences, for example, between areas like Cross Hands and Melksham, brought some amusing experiences from which we all learned so much. Then the involvement in the hotel and leisure sectors, of which we knew so little, must have seemed a bit like a helter-skelter ride for people like Terry Jones and Adrian Davies and all those loyal members of our team who have stuck with us throughout.

As we publish our story we are embarking on what will undoubtedly be the largest project ever for the Leekes team. The development of Hensol Castle and its adjoining buildings, the proposed rugby and football training academy, together with the existing Vale Resort, will create a facility of which we can be enormously proud.

However, the retail division still remains the cornerstone of our business and I anticipate we shall open our next store within a year or so, most likely in the Worcester area. I know from personal experience that the success of developments like these can only be achieved through the dedication of the team involved and I have been very fortunate to have had the very best helping me over the years. There are too many to mention in a short note like this but my gratitude to them all cannot be overstated.

Now, of course, to my own children – Emma, Stephen, Joanna and Christopher – who have chosen to join the business. They will all make their own marks and achievements, I have no doubt, in the years to come. Goodness knows what sort of organisation they, or perhaps even their children, may be running in, say, another 40 years' time. I often wonder what on earth my grandfather or father would make of it all if they came back for an update.

On a personal note, I have enjoyed my time enormously in every aspect of the business. I might have done a few things differently in the light of experience – but probably not much. I really don't envy young people today starting out on their own for the first time: the red tape, rules, regulations and legislation are making it increasingly difficult for new companies to succeed. I prefer to just pick up the phone and get on with it; probably not a style that endears anyone to the authorities these days.

My advice to anyone wishing to start their own business is simply not to be afraid of making your own judgements and decisions, and sometimes your own gut-feeling can well be a better guide than all the professional advice you could take. I've always had a great interest in sport and think the similarity with business is clear. You have to have some definite goals, do some research, be prepared for hard work but, foremost, be part of a good team. You can't play every position yourself even though you might like to!

If you have all that and just a little bit of luck from time to time you might even have a bit of fun in business as well! I'd like to think that was the case for everyone who has been a part of the Leekes story.

*Gerald Leeke*
*April 2007*